20—
1 35

MEDITATIONS ON MIDDLE-EARTH

MEDITATIONS ON MIDDLE-EARTH

EDITED BY KAREN HABER

A BYRON PREISS BOOK

ST. MARTIN'S PRESS
NEW YORK

Editor: Karen Haber
Project Editor: Howard Zimmerman
Designed by Gilda Hannah
Interior Illustrations copyright © John Howe 2001
Jacket illustration by John Howe
copyright © 2001 John Howe/Sophisticated Games, Ltd.

A BYRON PREISS BOOK

www.stmartins.com

ISBN 0-312-27536-6

First Edition: November 2001

10 9 8 7 6 5 4 3 2 1

In memory of Poul Anderson

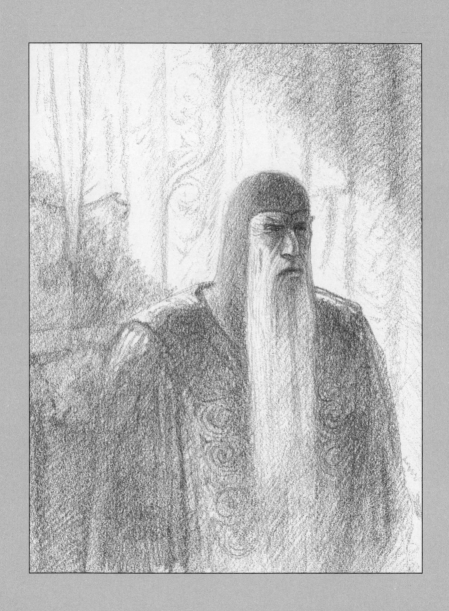

CONTENTS

PREFACE:
THE BEAT GOES ON

Now it can be told: I lived with an elf.

Actually, she was my college roommate. She had, in fact, a perfectly good birth name, but she chose to call herself "Arwen Evenstar," and put *that* name in the tin frame on the door to our room. Her boyfriend was, of course, "Strider." Despite his moniker he preferred drag racing to walking.

I was not as nice to her—or to him—as I could have been. Maybe I had elf issues. But I really didn't want to live with an elf, especially one who typed fan letters to Jerry Garcia at 2 A.M. on *my* typewriter.

Not that I had anything against J. R. R. Tolkien, you understand. Thirty-odd years ago I had, of course, read The Lord of the Rings. It was practically a rite of passage.

Tolkien surprised me. I hadn't expected to like his books. Hobbits? Wizards? Nevertheless, the power of his storytelling reached out, grabbed me, and would not let go. This was a bit dismaying. Here I was, a sophisticated high school sophomore, reading the same books as those contemptible little nerdy freshmen.

And yes, I felt the magic. Hated Sauron. Was disgusted by Gollum. I have to admit that I preferred Bilbo to Frodo; and Sam got on my nerves with all that unwavering loyalty. I had an even harder time with the heroic elves (see "elf issues," above). I was probably just a wee bit too old and hormonally activated to fall completely under the hobbits' spell. But I enjoyed the books.

I might have enjoyed them even more had I made the interesting connection between "hottie" elfs and Mr. Spock as Esther Friesner had (see her essay for the details). Speaking of odd "crossings in the field," does anyone else remember watching Leonard Nimoy—on a black-and-white TV, of course—crooning in a baritone only slightly deeper and more supple than Cher's, the lyrics to the song "Bilbo Baggins"? I remember a fragment about "the bravest little hobbit of them all . . ." It was a silly tune, and I was embarrassed to witness a sacred science-fiction icon making this unexpected trans-genre move. But there, for anyone with the ears, pointed or not, to hear, was the steady percussive influence of J. R. R. Tolkien infiltrating yet another aspect of pop culture.

Remember the *Harvard Lampoon* parody *Bored of the Rings*? This good natured on-target parody made riotous fun of Tolkien's heroes and villains. If I may lovingly quote two favorite giddy lines:

" 'Aiyee!' shouted Legolam. 'A Thesaurus!' "

" 'Maim!' roared the monster. 'Mutilate, mangle, crush. See HARM.' "

You must admit that the base material is powerful when even the parody continues to echo down the years.

Then I graduated from high school, was done with hobbits, and even *Star Trek*. Imagine, then, my surprise—and chagrin—when I met "Arwen." She was pretty, rather ethereal, with a lilting voice, and long pale hair. Come to think of it, she did make a convincing elf. (I never checked her ears, nor "Strider's.")

A mere twenty-five years later, latent karma has given me a chance to make amends for my cruelty to elves and their significant others by helming this collection of meditations about that seminal elfmeister, J. R. R. Tolkien, and the entity that is Lord of the Rings.

Aside from providing me with a college roommate dilemma, Tolkien set down the literary backbeat to my experimental reading years, circa 1968–1978. If you liked science fiction and fantasy—and I did—The Lord of the Rings was unavoidable.

With the sudden availability of paperback editions of The Lord of the Rings in the late 1960s, the demand for fantasy fiction reached tidal-wave proportions. The books had been kept out of paperback by the hardcover publisher, but once that ban was lifted, thousands of readers rushed into the bookstores, bought the trilogy, and cried for more. The hunger for fantasy fiction, once aroused, became—and remains—insatiable.

Publishers were not slow to notice. They, too, rushed: to find writers who could—and did—produce imitative trilogies. Soon the bookstores were flooded with huge hobbit-like tales, which also sold in amazing quantities. The rising tide began to float other, older, boats, among them Robert E. Howard's Conan novels, once a cult phenomenon, now a new literary phenomenon. To its everlasting credit, Ballantine Books, Tolkien's paperback publisher, brought out its Adult Fantasy series, edited by Lin Carter, which made the classic fantasy masterpieces by James Branch Cabell, Lord Dunsany, E. R. Eddison, and Mervyn Peake available to modern readers.

An entire subsidiary Tolkien industry sprouted like toadstools on a barrow log: calendars, tarot cards, games, postcard books, posters, audio cassettes, maps, movies. Soon it seemed that everybody wanted to sit in and jam with the master.

The beat goes on. If you look at the *New York Times* Bestseller List for any given week in any given month of the past two years, you will undoubtedly find at least one fantasy book there, usually in the top five. Harry Potter has been identified by many readers and critics as the direct descendant of Tolkien's literary line.

Readers wanted more, and they got it. For some of them, fantasy became not only an obsession but a lifestyle. For others, it became a career, as readers morphed into writers.

ꝂMAUG FLYING AROUND THE MOUNTAIN

The Hobbit

Chapter XII: "Inside Information"

Some began improvising upon Tolkien's rhythms and themes. And some went on to write their own fantasy symphonies.

Many writers have indeed left their own marks upon fantasy literature with profound, poignant, and even funny tales. To take just a sampling from the contributors to this book, consider Ursula Le Guin's Earthsea series, Terry Pratchett's tales of Discworld, Raymond E. Feist's Riftwar books, and Orson Scott Card's Legends of Alvin Maker. All of these writers have won huge followings for their work.

In the decades since The Lord of the Rings was first published as a mass-market paperback, we've seen some mighty fancy performances, some impressive riffs and solos; but regardless of how progressive or decadent the melody, the plain fact is that, if you listen carefully, you can still hear J. R. R. Tolkien back there, holding steady on the pulsing heartbeat of fantasy literature.

Tolkien's compelling story formulation was drawn from heroic myths and legends, and marked by his own distinct sense of language and verse. He didn't invent these themes, but he brought them together in a seamless progressive tale of such charm and power that here, many years later, we are gathered to do him honor.

It's a mark of the power of Tolkien's storytelling that so many writers feel passionately about his work, and are willing to discuss it in these pages. The essays offered here by masters of fantastic literature are literal meditations upon J. R. R. Tolkien and his influence on them as writers, and as readers, and upon the fantasy literature field as a whole. The comments range far, wide, and wondrous. You'll find affectionate memories, startling revelations, intriguing analyses, and heartstring-twanging sentiment.

George R. R. Martin discusses the hallmarks of epic—i.e., Tolkienesque-fantasy. Ursula K. Le Guin takes us right into the Master's technique with a compelling analysis of Tolkien's word rhythms. Terry Pratchett munches on the evolution of a cult favorite into a publishing phenomenon. Raymond Feist traces the emergence of the modern fantasy novel and his own discovery of fantasy literature. Poul Anderson recreates the lost world of 1950s and the impact of Tolkien's work in that cold war era. Diane Duane remembers the longest Sunday—and Monday—of her adolescent life, spent waiting to purchase the last book of the trilogy. The Brothers Hildenbrandt review the need to "edit" Gandalf's eyebrows. Terri Windling focuses on the metaphorical and healing uses of fantasy. Charles de Lint shares his discovery that magic promised a deeper connection with the actual world. Esther Friesner reveals for the first time the unsuspected connection between The Lord of the Rings and *Star Trek*. Harry Turtledove explains why Tolkien was bad for his academic career but good for his literary future. Robin Hobb brings us into an Alaskan meat cache, where she delved into Tolkien's work for the first time, and as a result found the direction that her own life would take. Lisa Goldstein ruminates on the changes in the fantasy field as other bards have taken up Tolkien's song. Michael Swanwick revisits the magic of Tolkien's books while reading them aloud to his young son. In addition to these meditations by fantasy writers, we offer an overview of Tolkien's work and its critcal reception by Tolkienist Douglas A. Anderson.

The point here is that, regardless of the particular writer/reader and his or her response, Tolkien touched them all, changed them, and changed fantasy literature as well. If you listen carefully now, you can still hear him, faintly, in the background. It's the rhythm to which an entire literary genre, its readers and its practitioners, has resonated for over thirty years. Come and join the dance.

—Karen Haber

P.S.: In case you're wondering what happened to "Arwen," all I can report is that she didn't return for sophomore year. I'll admit to a teeny guilt pang over that, although I don't think she was a good match for that particular educational institution. However, I really should have been nicer. Instead, as soon as possible, I switched roommates and spent the second half of my freshman year bunking with an earthy gal who liked to read mysteries and whose boyfriend reminded me of Gollum. Of course I was dating somebody who, in retrospect, could have passed for a Balrog, but that's another story. . . .

MEDITATIONS ON MIDDLE-EARTH

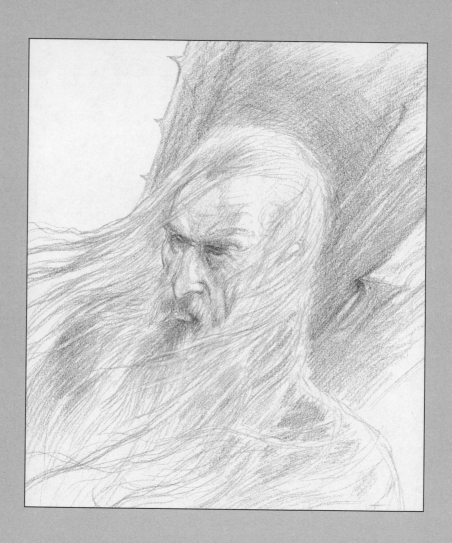

INTRODUCTION

GEORGE R. R. MARTIN

Fantasy existed long before J. R. R. Tolkien. There was never an age in human history when men did not wonder what might lie beyond the next hill, and fill the blank spaces on their maps with marvels and terrors. The first fantasist spun his tales squatting by a fire, as he shared a haunch of charred mastodon with his fellows. Homer was a fantasist, and Shakespeare was another.

Conan, that seminal barbarian of our times, would have been right at home quaffing a horn of mead with Siegfried and Beowulf.

Sir Thomas Malory and *Le Morte d'Arthur* came centuries before Tolkien. So did Théroulde's *Song of Roland*. Bram Stoker and Edgar Allen Poe did some splendid work on the borderlands between fantasy and horror, while William Morris created worlds vast and wondrous, distant precursors to Middle-earth.

In this century, Lord Edward Dunsany, James Branch Cabell, and E. R. Eddison each put his own stamp on the literature of fantasy. The importance of Robert Ervin Howard and his Hyborian Age cannot be overestimated, nor that of Fritz Leiber, who went Conan two better with his Fafhrd and the Grey Mouser. In a very different tradition one finds Gerald Kersh, John Collier, Thorne Smith, Abraham Merritt, and Clark Ashton Smith.

Even during his own lifetime, Tolkien had formidable rivals. While he was telling his tales of Middle-earth, his fellow Inkling C. S. Lewis was shaping Narnia. Elsewhere in England, Mervyn Peake was creating the great gloomy castle of Gormenghast, and across the sea in America the incomparable stylist Jack Vance was writing his first tales of the Dying Earth.

Yet it was Middle-earth that proved to have the greatest staying power. Fantasy had existed long before him, yes, but J. R. R. Tolkien took it and made it his own in a way that no writer before him had ever done, a way that no writer will ever do again. The quiet Oxford philologist wrote for his own pleasure, and for his children, but he created something that touched the hearts and minds of millions.

He introduced us to hobbits and Nazgûl, took us through the Misty Mountains and the mines of Moria, showed us the siege of Gondor and the Cracks of Doom, and none of us have ever been the same . . . especially the writers.

Tolkien *changed* fantasy; he elevated it and redefined it, to such an extent that it will never be the same again. Many different flavors of fantasy continue to be written and published, certainly, but one variety has come to dominate both bookstore shelves and bestseller lists. It is sometimes called epic fantasy, sometimes high fantasy, but it ought to be called Tolkienesque fantasy.

The hallmarks of Tolkienesque fantasy are legion, but to my mind one stands high above all the rest: J. R. R. Tolkien was the first to create a fully realized secondary universe, an entire world with its own geography and histories and legends, wholly unconnected to our own, yet somehow just as real. "Frodo Lives," the buttons might have said back in the sixties, but it was not a picture of Frodo that Tolkien's readers taped to the walls of their dorm rooms, it was a map. A map of a place that never was.

Tolkien gave us wondeful characters, evocative prose, some stirring adventures and exciting battles . . . but it is the *place* we remember most of all. I have been known to say that in contemporary fantasy the setting becomes a character in its own right. It is Tolkien who made it so.

Most contemporary fantasists happily admit their debt to the master (among that number I definitely include myself), but even those who disparage Tolkien most loudly cannot escape his influence. The road goes ever on and on, he said, and none of us will ever know what wonderous

BILBO WITH GOLLUM

The Hobbit

Chapter V: "Riddles in the Dark"

places lie ahead, beyond that next hill. But no matter how long and far we travel, we should never forget that the journey began at Bag End, and we are all still walking in Bilbo's footsteps.

OUR GRANDFATHER:

MEDITATIONS ON J. R. R. TOLKIEN

RAYMOND E. FEIST

If you've read a single fantasy novel in your life by anyone other than J. R. R. Tolkien, there's a better-than-even chance at least one reviewer has compared the writer under discussion to Tolkien. Or the jacket blurb, provided by someone in the publisher's publicity department, makes the comparison. It's a fact of publishing life, and has nothing to do with the style, ambitions, or the wishes of the author being reviewed or blurbed. Everyone gets compared to Tolkien.

Reviewers often like to use a well-known touchstone to inform their readers of the nature of the book under review. It's not uncommon to read a review where a mystery is compared to a work by Raymond Chandler, or a western is compared to the work of Louis L'Amour. I have, in turn, been damned by reviewers for being "too much like Tolkien" and for "not being enough like Tolkien." I'm not exaggerating; and the ironic fact is both those reviews were forwarded to me by my publisher on the same day.

Blurb writers often fall into the trap of using "not since J. R. R. Tolkien has a writer . . ." types of copy. It's easy, and it lets the potential reader of the book know what to expect: magic, derring-do, high adventure, etc.

Why all the constant comparison to J. R. R. Tolkien? Why is he the touchstone against which all of us in the fantasy field are struck to test our mettle? Simply put, he is considered by many to be the Father of Us All.

I disagree. From my point of view, Fritz Leiber was *my* spiritual father, along with any other number of writers who influenced my childhood: Sir Walter Scott, Robert Louis Stevenson, Rafael Sabatini, Anthony Hope, Samuel Shellabarger, Mary Renault, Thomas Costain, and others. For other fantasy writers it was H. P. Lovecraft, Edgar Rice Burroughs, Robert E. Howard, A. Merritt, or H. Rider Haggard; but Tolkien was our grandfather, no doubt. My view may be in the minority, but then again, I'm a minority of one in any event. But allow me the indulgence of giving you my reasons, and why I think, in the long run, that considering him our spiritual grandfather is a more respectful judgment for working authors today.

When I was a kid, my reading tastes were pretty thoroughly locked into what was then called "boys' adventure books," a curious offshoot from classical romances of the nineteenth century. I remember crouching under the covers with a flashlight when I was supposed to be sleeping, or hiding a dog-eared copy of some old novel in my notebook at school and trying to look studious. The teacher would drone on as I read *Captain Blood* by Sabatini, or *Castle Dangerous* by Scott. I remember devouring the entire Leatherstockings Saga by James Fenimore Cooper, and that experience stayed with me so long that when my publisher wanted a rubric for my first trilogy I came up with Riftwar Saga. My children will probably never understand the pleasure I took from those books. If they read any of those titles, they will most likely consider them "quaint."

The modern realism of the early twentieth century began the decline of this delicious genre. Film and television killed it.

Cooper could spend ten pages describing a one-room log cabin, because his contemporary readers wanted details. They lived in townhouses in Boston or London, and had never seen a cabin or river houseboat. The closest they had come to an indigenous native was the cigar store Indian outside their local tobacconist. The richness of the images provided by the narrator were a requirement for success. Today's readers have seen Davy Crockett and Daniel Boone reruns, and have no need for that sort of leisurely narrative and detailed description. They want action and dialogue, and they want it now.

As I grew up—I refuse to claim I matured—I discovered "classic" adventure literature—Twain, Cooper, Scott, then the "boys' adventure" writers. Later I chanced upon science fiction, then fantasy, and embraced them as the logical inheritors of this still-lamented genre. I even remember my introduction to science fiction and fantasy.

In the eighth grade I was required to compose a book report from a novel chosen from an approved list, books made available to my school by generous publishers via a Scholastic publication called "My Weekly Reader." The list was short and had a couple of Hardy Boys and Nancy Drew titles, as well as some other equally suspect fare; but one title drew my eye: *The Cycle of Fire* by Hal Clement. All I remember about the blurb was the word "adventure," and I believe "alien" and "space" were also employed. So I checked it off the page and about two weeks later it arrived.

I was hooked. Science fiction was exactly the high adventure fare I had become addicted to, as well as providing a more modern sensibility regarding ethics and morality. Characters weren't quite as noble as they were in Ivanhoe, nor were the issues of right and wrong always as clearly defined. But, boy, was there plenty of action and a lot of fun stuff that included spies, space battles, and huge empires. E. E. "Doc" Smith was a fair substitute for Sir Walter Scott or Robert Louis Stevenson in my boyish judgment. And by the time I got to Robert A. Heinlein and Isaac Asimov, I was no longer interested in knights in shining armor and pirates on the Spanish Main.

It was about 1966 when I discovered Tolkien. A friend lent me the Ace edition of *The Fellowship of the Ring*. I wasn't thrilled at first. The references to *The Hobbit*, and the rather leisurely pace of the first chapter, almost put me off. But there was a charm to the narrative; and while I didn't know who Bilbo or Gandalf were, I was willing to stick around and see what happened to them. After a while I discovered a wonderful nineteenth-century narrative style, and it occurred to me much later that J. R. R. Tolkien had also read "boys' adventure" novels as a youngster. His choice of style and pace was as if a favorite old uncle were reading me a wonderful tale of knights and quests.

Only the knights weren't champions of King Arthur's court; they were interesting little characters called hobbits, and their role in the destruction of the One Ring wasn't quite Percival and the Holy Grail.

When the Fellowship was destroyed, I put the first book down and said, "What's next?"

Off I went to the used bookstore I habituated, and there I found the second volume, *The Two Towers*. I also found *The Return of the King,* and decided to pick that up as well, as I figured I'd probably want to finish the entire story.

Within a day or so I had neglected my studies, and my other obligations, to plow through the final two volumes. I then went back to the bookstore and got *The Hobbit*. I didn't find it as sweeping or as grand a narrative as The Lord of the Rings, but it was fun.

So I went back to the store and said, "What else has he written?"

The answer was, "Nothing." I know now there were scholarly works and poetry, but this was an American used bookstore, remember. So I said, "What else have you got like this stuff?"

And this is how I came to know Robert E. Howard, A.

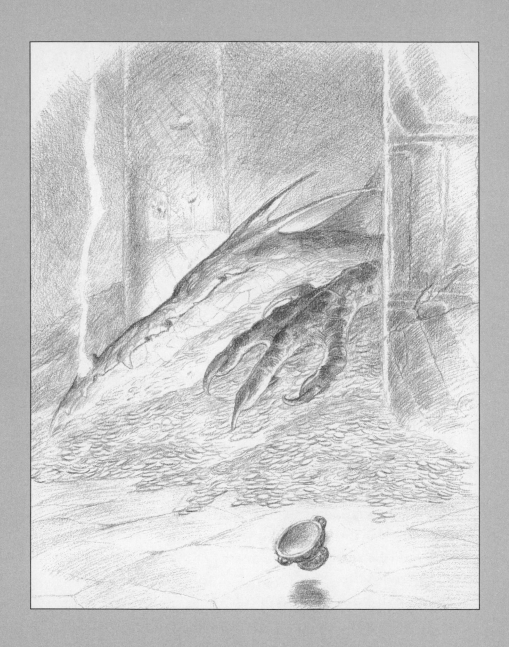

BILBO STEALS THE CUP

The Hobbit

Chapter XII: "Inside Information"

Merritt, H. Rider Haggard, and Fritz Leiber. I became as hooked on fantasy as I had been on science fiction.

What was it about The Lord of the Rings that hooked me? Foremost it was the classic motif of the underdog, the diminutive Frodo being the only stalwart to endure the breaking of the Fellowship. He, along with Sam, Meriadoc, and Pippin, were willing to brave tribulations that the larger, more "classic" heroic figures were unwilling to confront: the obvious evils of Sargon, the twisted ambition of Saruman, the tragic Gollum, and the insidious lure of the power of the One Ring itself.

This was classic stuff. This was right up there with Wagner's *Twilight of the Gods* and *Beowulf*. It was heroic in a fashion similar to the Arthurian stories of Malory and Tennyson, of the tales of the Mabinogion, yet with a decidedly modern patina.

Frodo is no one's first image of a "hero." Lancelot and Orlando would tower over him. He is gentle, like the rest of his kind, fond of food, drink, and comfort. In many respects, he is the surrogate for Tolkien's expected audience, the secure, well-educated, contented British upper-class and upper middle-class readers of the pre–World War II era.

Much scholarly enquiry has gone into the cautionary aspects of Lord of the Rings as a metaphor of Britain's travails before and during World War II. This resonates across time as Frodo, the "everyman" of the saga confronts the mounting evil threatening his native soil. He and his companions return home as heros after the destruction of the One Ring, and that heroism and its impact is demonstrated by the cleansing of the Shire; no timid little men here, but battle-hardened veterans who take things in hand and free their homes of the domestic tyrants who have come to plague their families while the heroes were saving the world.

It was delicious and compelling and a story that demanded rereading time and again.

And how did it impact me as a writer?

First of all, indirectly. The world of Midkemia, in which the preponderance of my work is set, is a gaming world, that is, one created by my friends in college as an environment in which we could play our personal variant of Dungeons & Dragons. As such, it's got a lot of "Tolkien stuff" in it. Orcs, for example, along with Balrogs, to name two clear-cut lifts. For the purposes of the books I've written in Midkemia, I've omitted most of the obvious critters that originated with Tolkien, but the influence, the "flavor" lingers.

Midkemia has elves and dwarves, like Middle-earth, but with my own peculiar twist on them. My elven races are a little more rawbone, less mystical than Tolkien's, and my dwarves bear far more resemblance to the hard-working Scottish coal miners who settled in western Pennsylvania than they do to dwarves in Middle-earth. My choice was for less mythic, more recognizably human variants of his prototypes; and I'm content with my choice, but I chose names right out of Tolkien's lexicon on the language of elves, in the *Silmarillion*. Elves of light are eledhel, dark elves are moredhel, to cite two borrowings. It was my "tip of the hat" to the grand old master.

For me, as a working writer, the major influence of J. R. R. Tolkien on my work was his impact on the publishing industry. He is the source of all wealth from which my bounty flows.

Before Tolkien, there were no international bestsellers written by fantasy authors, at least not in the sense we think of "bestseller" today.

The success of The Lord of the Rings began slowly, and crested in the late 1960s and early 1970s. Looking back, we can now see it as a monolithic, time-compressed "event," marked by the publication of the *Silmarillion*. If memory serves, the brilliant promotion by Random House/Del Rey books at the time created a demand for an American "first edition," which resulted in a print run of around a million copies in the United States alone.

This was an heroic feat of publishing in the mid-1970s. It was followed by calendars, art books, other merchandizing tie-ins, a TV special, films, and the rest. The Middle-earth franchise is today one of *Star Wars* proportions. It was not always thus.

A slow, word-of-mouth growth, mostly on college campuses, was what I remember about The Lord of the Rings in the late 1960s. For a while it was almost a sign of being "hip" that you'd read the trilogy, because the books weren't mainstream bestsellers.

They were, to put it simply, cool.

But today my success is to a large degree the result of that desire by scattered college students, hippies, and fans of literature to read something that was "cool." To be able to go to that party where the jocks and frat guys weren't going to show up, and to talk about that "cool" story, The Lord of the Rings.

More than the works of those authors I've named above,

J. R. R. Tolkien's brilliantly realized story of Frodo and his companions sparked an appetite for fantasy that led to many writers being "discovered" by readers who had missed them the first time around.

Lin Carter had edited a series for Random House under the Ballantine Adult Fantasy banner, with works by James Branch Cabell and Lord Dunsany, among others, and suddenly they were flying out of the used bookstores, eagerly devoured by the newly converted fantasy buffs. The great writers of "pulp" fantasy, A. Merritt, H. Rider Haggard, George Sylvester Viereck and Paul Eldridge, Robert E. Howard, as well as Arthur Conan Doyle's Professor Challenger books, and the non-Tarzan work of Edgar Rice Burroughs, were embraced decades after their original publication due to the thirst for fantasy created by J. R. R. Tolkien.

Of those writers, Robert E. Howard enjoyed a renascence that ended up surpassing his original modest success in manyfold fashion, as his Conan stories found new readership; spawned follow-up works by no less a pair of talents than L. Sprague De Camp and Robert Jordan; and created its own franchise, including two films and a TV series. And my personal hero, Fritz Leiber, found new readers for his Fafhrd and the Gray Mouser stories.

But the tales of lost civilizations, ancient gods, and wandering barbarians lacked the grandeur and mythic underpinnings of Tolkien. Certainly, H. P. Lovecraft's stories of the Ancient Ones dealt with centuries-spanning evil, lurking below the surface of our mundane world, but the conflicts were always on a personal scale, a poor soul who by circumstances found himself confronting horrors beyond imagining. And there were never stories of triumph, merely of surviving the confrontation.

H. Rider Haggard and A. Merritt wrote of great civilizations, but they were always fallen, discovered centuries later by contemporary characters of the early twentieth century who were confronting timeless evils, immortal goddesses or spirits in possession of their fellow explorers.

Only Burroughs got close with his John Carter stories, but even the heroic former Confederate officer transported to Mars, with its seven-foot-tall, six-armed Martians, and exotic princesses, was still not in the same category as Tolkien. This was still clearly "pulp" fantasy.

Tolkien stood alone atop the publishing pyramid when it came to fantasy. He had contemporaries of worth—E. R. Eddison, T. H. White, and C. S. Lewis—but somehow Tolkien had hit the mark with his mix of lore, ancient back story, and characters.

His Third Age, his "Myth for Britain," echoed with reverberations of ancient majesty. That oddest of beings, a British christian mystic, Tolkien possessed personal beliefs that clearly influenced his cosmology, the sense of ultimate good and evil, the timeless conflict, and the temptations of dark powers luring even the most innocent and pure. Yet it was clear that in the end, good would be triumphant.

While the pulp writers of the 1920s and 1930s dealt with modern man blundering into dangers and terrors of ancient origin, exploring lost tombs in the heart of ancient jungles or buried under the shifting sands of remote deserts, Tolkien changed that paradigm. He created a world both alien and familiar. The Shire was "home." No matter that the reader lived far from the green meadows of the West Counties of England, or had never seen the sunset from the banks of the Thames, the Shire felt like home.

Frodo and the hobbits were "people," simple, graceful, peaceful, and humble. They were archetypes bordering on stereotypes: Frodo the Plucky Hero, Sam the Good and Faithful, Gandalf the eminence who could not possibly be more grise, Merry and Pippin, as hale a pair of well-met fellows as you'd find in Percival C. Wren's *Beau Geste* or Alexander Dumas's *The Three Musketeers*, uncertain as to why they were a part of the drama but willing to put aside personal safety for friendship. They were two of my favorites in the series, two callow youths who found strength and purpose through adversity and who emerged as heros.

Tom Bombadil, the Ents, the Nazgûl, the Balrog, and the elves were the otherworldly entities within the structure of that universe that created a supernatural element in an already fanciful story. Even the human characters were made somehow alien so that the hobbits could be realized as all the more familiar to the reader.

It's all there, heroism and humility, fear and triumph, a mysterious king returning to rule with wisdom and generosity, a princess destined to fight alongside her betrothed; it's stuff right out of Richard Wagner.

This wondrous story created an appetite in readers for future works of truly epic proportion. While it's an overused word in ad copy, "epic" in this context is well used, for The Lord of the Rings is a story of profound changes within a culture/society as a result of the tale. The hobbits will never quite be the same, and we can see the foreshadowing of the coming of the Fourth Age, the one we assume Tolkien meant to be our own.

My own work is more character-driven, with contemporary "actors" in costume, as it were. But the backdrop of my universe's cosmology, the titanic struggle between ancient gods, is as large a back story as Tolkien's. It runs through every book I write, sometimes a major part of the narrative, other times as a distant echo, but always there.

That desire for the Wagnerian, the grand opera, as opposed to the grand guignol of Robert E. Howard and H. P. Lovecraft, was the single most tangible legacy to me, as a writer, from Tolkien. I'll leave it to posterity to decide if I've met the test.

In any event, no matter how we get there, we're all obliged to admit that while Tolkien may not have truly been "the father" of modern heroic fantasy, he was certainly the grandfather, and as such his direct influences on style, readership, and market were in many ways more important to my career than the direct influences of other writers might have been to my writing. In my own humble opinion, of course.

So while I'll point to the others as being my spiritual "fathers," especially to Fritz, I'll once again tip my hat to J. R. R. Tolkien as being our collective, spiritual grandfather.

Thanks, Granddad. I couldn't have done it without you.

AWAKENING THE ELVES

⊃⊂

POUL ANDERSON

We are all deeply in J. R. R. Tolkien's debt, writers perhaps even more than readers. He gave us the greatest fantasy of our time, which also stands tall in the whole of world literature. Only Lord Dunsany is comparable, and Tolkien's influence has been vastly stronger.

Both drew on our literary and cultural wellsprings, from

Homer and the Bible onward. A little more about that anon. First I'd like to reminisce a bit. The aim is not to brag, but to offer a personal example of how that influence has worked. Many other people must have such stories to tell, in wide variety, and I hope that some of them do.

Back in the early 1950s, my wife and I met the late Reginald Bretnor and his own wife. It led to a lot of lively conversations, with considerable benefit to the California wine industry, and a friendship that endured through her untimely death, until his, eight or nine years ago. The friendship grew close enough that he not only told us about *The Hobbit* but lent us his first-edition copy. Thereupon we had to find one for ourselves, and presently, having heard about The Lord of the Rings, acquire and devour it.

That was the initial English publication, three volumes appearing over a period of more than a year. The time felt longer. Readers today may have trouble imagining what that was like—waiting months to learn how Frodo and Sam fared in the Land of Shadow, then months again wondering what would happen to Frodo in the hands of the enemy!

(This led to the common mistake of calling The Lord of the Rings a trilogy. It isn't. It's a unified novel, issued in pieces for commercial reasons.)

Even so, we were not alone in our enthusiasm. People discussed it eagerly at science fiction conventions. The songs were set to music and sung, like those in that other splendid fantasy, John Myers Myers' *Silverlock*. It is actually a sign of esteem and affection that a very funny ballad version, "The Orcs' Marching Song," evolved; it goes to the tune of "Jesse James."

Thus, word got around. In those days, the paperback

house Ace Books was under entirely different ownership and management from now. The United States had not yet joined the International Copyright Convention, and indeed copyright law generally was in sore need of amendment. Ace saw a broad loophole, and put out an American soft-cover edition without so much as a by-your-leave.

This raised indignation among those who realized what it meant; but they were few compared to the ordinary readers who in all good faith bought the volumes. Tolkien spoke to the young people of the sixties—with images of peace and natural beauty, their desecration, the struggle of a dauntless handful against an evil that looked over-whelming—and, to be sure, glamor, strangeness, a narra-tion that grabbed hold and didn't let go till the end, a whole world so fully and vividly imagined that it felt altogether real.

Oh, yes, these remarks are truisms, and barely graze the whole truth. The Lord of the Rings is far more. It deals with questions fundamental and timeless, the nature of good and evil, of man, and of God. Because of that, over and above its sheer readability, it endures, and undoubtedly will en-dure, as the plays of Shakespeare, or *Alice in Wonderland,* or *The Adventures of Huckleberry Finn,* do and will.

Whatever respect I had had for Edmund Wilson evapo-rated when, at windy length, he dismissed The Lord of the Rings as childish. Granted, my opinion of critics never was especially high. "They who can, do. They who can't, teach. They who can't even teach become critics." In fairness, it must be admitted that several of Wilson's colleagues saw the matter otherwise, and today Tolkien is fully accepted by the literary establishment.

THE THREE TROLLS TURNED TO STONE

The Hobbit

Chapter II: "Roast Mutton"

This crotchet of mine is beside the point. Let's get back to events.

The rip-off didn't make me indignant, it made me god-damn furious. I vowed in the hearing of friends that Ace would publish nothing more by me until the issue had been settled to the satisfaction of Professor Tolkien. This was put to the test when the company made me a reprint proposal. My then hardback publisher, Doubleday, although entitled to half the payment, went along with my refusal. I like to think that this added some slight force to the pressure on Ace. It's an amusing footnote that shortly afterward another softcover house tendered my agent a higher bid on the same book.

Be this as it may, Ace eventually gave in and made a settlement, which included turning American rights over to well-regarded Ballantine Books. To secure the copyright, Tolkien did a few revisions of his text. I'm not sure what they were, but they can't be important. Since then, The Lord of the Rings has never been out of print.

Another footnote: I declared peace with Ace, and they took a couple more of my books—*faute de mieux* on both sides—before the firm was acquired by Tom Doherty. He's a highly ethical man, who among other things paid authors half a million dollars in royalties that an audit showed had gone unreported when due, in spite of being under no legal requirement to do so. Ace again bears an honorable name.

Naturally, the success of The Lord of the Rings led to a revival of *The Hobbit* and of everything else Tolkien wrote— aside from strictly scholarly papers, and maybe they too have become readily available. Some is profound, some is utter delight, and some, frankly, leaves me a little cold. This merely shows that Tolkien's work ranges more widely than my mind, and I needn't bore you with specifics.

Equally naturally, The Lord of the Rings roused a fresh interest in out-and-out fantasy. That interest had always existed. Likely the first stories ever told were fantasies. Besides Ung, the caveman's account of the big one that got away, humans must have wondered about the world, its days and nights, seasons and creatures, life, birth, death, luck, love, all the mysteries. They had nothing but imagination to help them try to understand. So arose religion, the magical arts, and folklore.

At least since Homer, probably earlier and certainly not only in the West, until recent times, fantasy was the mainstream of literature. Granted, "realistic" stories, that is, stories without anything in them that we today consider impossible, also go far back. They became the dominant and most reputable sort in the course of the nineteenth century, when an ascending bourgeoisie was more interested in reading about itself than about faerie lands forlorn. (No reverse snobbery here. After all, the genre includes many such works as *War and Peace.* Furthermore, it isn't absolutely distinct from fantasy. Where, for example, would you place *Moby Dick*?)

Quite a few authors, writing about the here and now still did occasional fantasies. To name just one, Rudyard Kipling's are among his finest creations. Several, such as James Branch Cabell, are remembered chiefly for their works of this kind. E. R. Eddison's first appeared in the 1920s, and *Silverlock,* already mentioned, did in 1949. Nonetheless, however much appreciated by connoisseurs, they gathered no large following. (*Jurgen* did, but as a *succès de scandale,* and nothing else by the author enjoyed anything like those sales in that brief moment.) *The Saturday Evening Post,* weekly voice of the middle class, published almost no fantasy unless by Stephen Vincent Benét. And so on.

Even markets catering to the imaginative devoted themselves mainly to science fiction, or at any rate what they could label science fiction. This was not the sea change one might think. During his editorship of *The Magazine of Fantasy and Science Fiction,* Anthony Boucher once remarked to me that, to judge by the mail he got, most of his readers preferred fantasy to science fiction, but didn't know it. You can, for instance, in terms of present-day scientific knowledge, make a somewhat better case for a life after death, and at least one God than you can for the possibility of time travel or travel faster than light.

In other words, the reading public kept an unexpressed desire for pure fantasy. And then Tolkien burst upon the publishing world. The rest is history.

The revival included what its devotees call heroic fantasy. In this, heroes, usually male but occasionally female, do battle against terrible odds in an archaic setting. That setting may be historical, but is most often imaginary; there has been no scientific or industrial revolution; supernatural forces and beings are real. Eddison wrote it on a high level, Robert E. Howard for the pulps. As always, borderline cases occur, for exmple, certain stories by L. Sprague De Camp and/or Fletcher Pratt, but I shan't elaborate on those except to give these particular ones my highest recommendation.

The Lord of the Rings is heroic fantasy. It is much else as well, but such elements are definitely integral to it. Its astonishing popularity revealed the latent demand for more. Supply was quickly forthcoming, and has been pour-ing out ever since.

We can pass by the derivatives, the derivatives of the derivatives, and whatnot, stuff that has prompted the scornful term "generic." They have been hilariously sati-rized by Esther Friesner and Diana Wynne Jones, among others. Let's simply recall Theodore Sturgeon's dictum, "Ninety percent of *everything* is crud," and judge the field by its best rather than its worst, as we judge the love story by *Romeo and Juliet* rather than by the soap operas. First-rate work has been and is being done in it.

Some old-timers have benefited, too, perhaps most no-tably Jack Vance and Robert Silverberg. Now let me get personal again, because my experience leads back to Tol-kien himself.

Long, long ago, I think probably in 1948, I wrote a heroic fantasy novel, *The Broken Sword,* which drew on Northern myth, saga, and folklore. Editor after editor rejected it, a few with regret, because they didn't believe it could sell. At last it found a publisher, who gave it one printing—coin-cidentally, in 1954, the same year that *The Fellowship of the Ring* came out—and let it die.

The post-Tolkien boom enabled the late Lin Carter to reprint a series of older fantasies with Ballantine. Among them eventually was *The Broken Sword.* Having meanwhile learned more about writing and, for that matter, medieval combat, I took the opportunity to revise it—same story but, I hoped, better told. The new version first appeared in 1971. Subsequently, I've been free to roam the fantasy field when-ever I like. That's a reason close to home for acknowledging a debt to Tolkien.

A major source of his was identical with mine. He drew on others as well, especially the Bible and Christian tradition. More about that later. Still, in his professorial capacity he was a scholar and translator of Old and Middle English literature. His long essay "On Fairy-stories" explores the meaningfulness and power of the folk tales from that era, which likewise inspired him.

His orcs and trolls come straight out of the North. I don't think his elves do, quite, and this seems worth examining.

I return to *The Broken Sword* only for comparison. Elves and trolls figure in it too. In fact, the story turns on a war between them. But these elves are very different, a difference that Tolkien would immediately have recognized.

Let me paraphrase my introduction to the revised edition. In the year 1018, the skald Sighvat Thordarson made a winter journey into Sweden at the behest of his lord, King Olaf of Norway, afterward known as St. Olaf. Most of Sweden was then pagan. Seeking overnight shelter, Sighvat was turned away from three successive homesteads—behavior extraordinary in that day and age, with religious cause. As he related in a poem he made about it:

> "That Odin be not angered,
> keep off!" the woman said.
> "We're heathen here and holding
> a holy eve, you wretch!"
> The carline who unchristianly
> cast me from the garth
> gave out that they would offer
> at evening to the elves.

The sagas mention other sacrifices to them, and a law that warships approaching a friendly shore must dismount their ferocious figureheads, lest the land-wights take offense.

Thus we see that they began as local gods or demi-gods. The *Heimskringla* tells of a petty king in a region of what was not yet Norway, buried with lavish grave-goods in a huge barrow. He came to be looked on as a tutelary spirit, given offerings and the posthumous name Olaf Geirstad-Elf. Legends about Elf Hill must spring from such happenings.

The Eddas speak of "light" and "dark" elves, though rather vaguely. It seems as if at least some of the light elves served in Asgard, and the dark ones may have been the dwarves—who are themselves prominent in Tolkien. But this may be the invention of poets and yarn-spinners in the Christian era, who continued for two or three centuries to use the old motifs. In any case, it has little to do with the concept of elves either as godlings or as roughly equivalent to classical dryads and oreads or Japanese kami.

They meant much to the early Germanic peoples. Probably they were far more real and immediate to most dwellers on heaths and lonely farms than were the great gods, of whom these outliers may well have heard only fragmentarily, if at all. Traces of their importance linger in names; for example, "Alfred" means "elf counsel."

Now, pagan gods were originally as ruthless as the natural forces and mortal conflicts they embodied. Homer, in the edited form we have him, and Hesiod can't entirely cover this up. For instance, we see Achilles slaughtering Trojan captives at the funeral of Patroclus, both to honor

him and to get help for him in the Otherworld. Human sacrifices were sometimes made directly to Odin, Thor, and
Frey. The elves lived on in folk belief long after the con-
version to Christianity. They kept the ancient heartless-
ness and trickiness. And so, in the medieval Danish ballad
"Elfshot," when a knight comes upon their moonlit dance
and declines to join it, he returns home a dying man.

It was this idea of the elves to which I harked back,
beautiful, entrancing, pleasure-loving, richly rewarding
their human favorites—as in the border ballad of True
Thomas—but ultimately without souls or much if any compassion.

As the centuries passed, they became ever less formidable. By the time of Elizabeth I, they were the impulsive
but civilized fays of *A Midsummer Night's Dream,* and by
the time of Victoria, they had shrunk to cutesy-poo mani-
kins. However, those of us who love the Northern tradition
remember what they once were.

Tolkien drew on it himself, not in mere imitation but
creatively. He kept trolls and orcs unsympathetic. He made
the dwarves less ambiguous, more reliably helpful, than
they are in the old stories. The elves underwent a complete
transfiguration.

Of course he knew exactly what he was doing, and succeeded nobly. His elves are as real as everybody else in the
epic, grave and brave, powerful and poetic, wonder-working
and wistful, an unattainable yet incontestable ideal. In my
opinion, here his source was most clearly the Bible, and he
was expressing his own faith. As my wife Karen says, these
elves are like seraphim.

Scholars, including him, have found that *Beowulf* is not a pagan tale with monkish glosses, but profoundly Christian from start to finish, even though set in an earlier era. Nine-fingered Frodo can stand side by side with Grendel's bane.

A CHANGELING RETURNS

MICHAEL SWANWICK

Not that many years ago, when the world was young and all things were as perfect as they were allowed to be, my nine-year-old son, Sean, demanded that I read to him The Lord of the Rings. His friend John Grant, it seems, had already heard it all the way through, and since John was only eight, Sean was suffering a major loss of prestige. Very well, I said, we'll start at bedtime. And so, for a long and magical run of nights, I journeyed together with my son through the great three-volumed world of Middle-earth.

It was not my first voyage there.

A quarter century before, in my high school days, my sister Patricia sent home from nursing school a box of paperbacks (I can see that box now, freshly opened and full of promise) which she had read and no longer wanted. Among them was *The Fellowship of the Ring*. I picked it up late one evening, after finishing my homework, meaning to read a chapter or two before sleep. I stayed up all night. It wasn't easy, but by skipping breakfast in the morning and reading every step of the way to school, I managed to finish the last page just as the bell rang for my first class to begin.

Oh, how that book shook and rattled me! It rang me like a bell. Even today, when I am three times as old as I was then, I can still hold my breath and hear the faint reverberations from that long, eternal night. That reading made me a writer, though it took me forever to learn my craft. It showed me what literature could do and what it could be.

Decades later, I wrote a story in homage to Tolkien, called "The Changeling's Tale." In it, a young tavern boy is swept up by a troupe of passing elves and carried away from hearth and home and all he knows and cares about. He pays a heavy price for the going, but he goes out of love for their beauty, their grace, and their strangeness, into a future of which all he can know is that it's beyond his imagining. It was an honest story, I hope. But it also carried an autobiographical weight. Will Taverner was as close as I will ever come to a self-portrait. His story is not that different from mine. Long ago, I ran away with the elves, and I never came back.

I reread The Lord of the Rings with trepidation. This book had shaped and formed me. What if it turned out to be only a minor work, just the first in the endless flood of interchangeable high-fantasy trilogies that have since inundated the bookstore racks? What if all my life had been the mere playing out of a childish enthusiasm?

All this I recounted during a panel on fantasy at I forget which convention. The audience was full of faces my own age, hair beginning to turn gray, bodies perhaps a little thicker than they once were. Many of them looked apprehensive. They, too, had been afraid to return to Middle-earth. And when I told them of my discovery, that it was still an important work and one that an adult could safely revisit, I saw those faces bloom with smiles of gratitude and relief.

But Sean did not hear the same book as the one I read to him.

What he heard was the same book I had discovered that sleepless night in the land of Long Ago and Far Away—the single best adventure story ever written. As an adult, however, I found that during my long absence it had transformed itself into something else entirely. It was now the saddest book in the world.

This is a tale in which everyone is in the process of losing everything they hold most dear. The elves, emblematic of magic, are passing away from Middle-earth. Galadriel laments the dwindling of Lothlorien. Treebeard reveals that ents are surrendering their awareness and growing increasingly tree-ish. The old ways—all of them—are disappearing. Trees are being cut down, and streams defiled. Blasting powder has been invented. Industrialization is on its way. Defeating the Dark Lord and slaughtering his armies will not change any of this.

Tolkien was quite rightly scornful of those who tried to read allegorical intent in his work. But absence of allegory does not equal lack of relevance. The critic Hugh Kenner has made a convincing case that *Waiting for Godot* began as a tale of two members of the French Resistance who, disguised as hobos, are sent on a dangerous journey across occupied countryside, and find their contact delayed. Fearful, in great peril, and unsure of the importance of their mission, they can only wait and bicker. If this theory is true, then Beckett systematically removed all specific signifiers from the play, and in the process made the plight of his two heroes universal. Restoring the literal origins of the story would only diminish it.

Similarly, to read Sauron as Hitler and the Ring as the atom bomb is to reduce a significant work to triviality. Yet Tolkien fought in World War I and he wrote much of his masterpiece during the darkest reaches of the second. The England of his youth was thoroughly gone by then. Like most of his generation, he mourned its passing. His portrayal of evil events was informed by things he knew only too well: Hitler, Mussolini, Stalin, the bomb, genocide, gas warfare, cultural homogenization, the Corporate State, depersonalization, pollution, mind control, the Big Lie . . . all the ills of his times are implicit in his work.

From experience, Tolkien knew that there are only two possible responses to the ending of an age. You can try to hold on, or you can let go. Those who try to seize the power to ward off change are corrupted by despair (Saruman, Theoden, and Denethor most notably, but there are others). Those who are willing to pay for all they have, to suffer and make sacrifices, to toil selflessly and honorably, and then to surrender their authority over what remains, ultimately gain the satisfaction of knowing that the world has a future worth passing on to their children. But it has no place for them anymore. Nevertheless—and this is what moved me most—Tolkien's vision of the combined horrors of the twentieth century ended with hope and forgiveness.

This is a book sad with wisdom. It moved me in ways my son could not feel.

You grow older, you grow more wary. As a boy in Vermont, I spent almost every day of one summer fishing in the Winooski River. I didn't tell my parents that my favorite spot was a backwater just below the hydroelectric dam at the head of a stretch of river bounded by high, steep cliffs to either side, which we all called the Gorge. The river churned wildly as it went through the Gorge, and every few years a teenager died falling from the cliffs. And I *certainly* didn't tell my parents that the way to the backwater was through the old power plant, and that it involved scrambling down the jagged, rusted-out remains of iron stairways, and taking a running leap over a gap that would have, at a minimum, broken bones if I'd slipped. For all that, those long summer days spent with my best friend Steve, fishing and talking and playing cards and reading stacks of comic books from each other's knapsacks, were one of the best times of my life. I wouldn't trade the memory of them for anything.

I shudder, though, to imagine my son risking his life the

THE RAVEN AND THOREN

The Hobbit

Chapter XV: "The Gathering of Clouds"

way I did clambering through the power plant. Or racing leapfrog across the wrecked cars in the automobile junkyard at the edge of town. Or breaking into abandoned houses to explore their spooky interiors. Or getting into rock-fights. Or going out onto the reservoir, as I did every year when the ice was beginning to melt and there was open water at its center, and jumping up and down to see how much of the ice could be made to sag under the water without my actually breaking through and drowning. Or . . . well, things look different when you're a grown-up. I couldn't understand them then, and I despair of explaining us now.

Nobody suggests that Bilbo go on the Ring-quest, though he stands up and volunteers to do so. On the evidence of *The Hobbit,* it might even seem that the quest is his by right. But he is, quite simply, too old, not only physically but spiritually as well. He has drunk of the wine of mortality, and for him the age of adventures is over.

So another hero must be found.

"You were *meant* to have it," Gandalf tells Frodo, unlikeliest of saviors. A string of coincidences brings the One Ring to him. It falls from the finger of a king, and is found by one scavenger and stolen by another. An adventurer, lost and seeking to evade orcs, chances upon it in the lightless passages beneath a mountain. A wizard convinces the adventurer to bequeath it to his nephew. The Ring, we are told, is actively seeking its master, Sauron. Yet its journey takes it directly away from Mordor, and straight to the Shire.

Coincidences multiply during Frodo's flight from Hobbiton. He leaves at the last possible instant, saved from a

Black Rider by the simple chance that the Gaffer thinks he's already left town. He is saved again by elves, who happen along just in the nick of time. He is saved a third time from Old Man Willow, and a fourth time from the barrow-wraiths by Tom Bombadil, who rather pushes plausibility by happening along just in the nick of time *twice*. In Bree, he is saved by Strider, who also happens along, again, just in the nick of time. At the Ford of Bruinen, he is saved by Elrond and Gandalf, who . . . well, you know the drill. There is a special providence on Frodo, guiding and protecting him all the way to Rivendell.

Yet from Rivendell onward, the quest is thwarted and delayed with maddening regularity. The Fellowship cannot take the pass through the Misty Mountains, and must therefore make the more perilous passage through Moria. Gandalf falls doing battle with a Balrog, depriving them of his strength and council. There are orcs on the eastern bank of the Anduin, forcing Frodo and Sam to travel downriver, away from their desired route. Gollum leads them up a road they cannot possibly survive.

But the contradiction is only apparent. There is a power at work here, both in the abetting and in the hindrance, "beyond any design of the Ring-maker," as Gandalf says. And there is on Middle-earth only one such power, though (significantly), it is never named.

Tolkien was religious, not in the loud, proselytizing manner of his friend C. S. Lewis (whom, to his frustration, he converted from atheism to Anglicanism, one crucial step short of Catholicism and salvation), but with the bone-deep sincerity of a man born into the faith he still holds. Which is to say, he was not trying to argue anyone to his beliefs, but only to portray the workings of the world as he understood them.

If we ask why an omnipotent and benevolent deity would put our hero through so much suffering in order to destroy the One Ring, we are asking the wrong question. For the mere destruction of evil was never on the agenda at all. Little children, in their frightening innocence, believe the world would be a better place if only we would kill all the bad people. Those adults who love them understand that the moral realm is more difficult than that, and that the evil we must fear the most resides within ourselves.

There's a subtler purpose at work here.

Ignore the geopolitics and the movements of armies, and follow instead the Ring as it travels toward its ultimate destiny. Time after time, Frodo unwittingly uses it to test those he encounters. First he offers the Ring to Gandalf, who, horrified, cries "No!" and "Do not tempt me!" Then he must rebuff the unwise desire of his beloved uncle and mentor Bilbo to hold it again. When Aragorn of the many names reveals his lineage, Frodo cries, "Then it belongs to you!" He offers it outright to Galadriel, who says to him, "Gently are you revenged for my testing of your heart at our first meeting;" and then, in one of the most memorable scenes in the book, proceeds to scare the snot out of him, before concluding, "I pass the test. I will diminish, and go into the West, and remain Galadriel." Boromir tries to seize it by force, but afterward redeems himself, according to his rough warrior's code, by dying in defense of the Fellowship. Boromir's brother Faramir, brashly declares that he would not pick it up if he found it lying in the road, and then, more nobly, proceeds to demonstrate the truth of his words. Denethor, who never gets within snatching distance of the thing, rhapsodizes on what he would do with it. In Mordor, the temptation is put first to Gollum, then to Sam, and ultimately to Frodo himself.

Frodo travels through Middle-earth like some kind of God-sent integrity test. The Wise, if they were truly so, upon seeing that he had come to visit, would shriek, "Oh, no! It's that fucking hobbit! I'm not in!" and slam the door in his face.

Here is the true purpose of the Ring-quest: not to destroy the source of power, but to test all of creation and decide whether it is worthy of continuance. Frodo's quest, though he doesn't know it, is a scouring of Middle-earth.

What's most interesting about the testing is that Frodo fails it.

What an *odd* protagonist Frodo turns out to be! He starts out well enough. The Lord of the Rings begins as a children's book and the sequel to a children's book, and through the first half of *The Fellowship of the Ring* struggles to emerge from its own failings, ranging from the unconvincing comic relief of the bumptious rustics to the twee insistence that hobbits are still among us, too quick and shy to be seen. Still, there are cunning bits of craft worked in there. Cleverly slipped into the creaking machinery surrounding Bilbo's "eleventeenth" birthday is the information that it is also Frodo's first day as an adult.

Okay, I was an English major. I know what a *bildungsroman* is. The coming-of-age novel has a venerable and well-known structure, and initially Frodo looks to be fulfilling it. He starts out cheerful, brave, resolute, and more than a little naive. When his duty is made clear to him, he stands up and, though with shrinking heart, unflinchingly accepts it.

But then, as he travels deeper into the heart of the matter, headed for Mordor, that perpetual dark night of the soul, he grows more and more passive, falls more and more silent. The business, for good and ill, of being the protagonist is perforce shouldered by his two talkative (they are needed to distract from his silence) companions, Sam and Gollum.

Sam and Gollum are interesting characters. But they are not completely comprehensible unless you realize that they are both aspects of Frodo. Taken in isolation, Sam is simply too good to be believed. He never shirks, never sulks, never gives a single thought to himself, unless it's of reproach for not having done well enough. His every action is motivated by love. He is (or becomes) the externalization of all that is best in Frodo. He fulfills the arc of growth a *bildungsroman* requires. Samwise Gamgee, the child who ran away from home hoping to see an oliphaunt, returns to the Shire as a man with the strength and decency needed to take his place in the community, and raise a family.

Where Sam is the Good Boy, Gollum is the Bad. It is not mere coincidence that Gollum is himself a fallen hobbit, nor that he and Sam unfalteringly hate each other. He has the Ring-bearer's determination, resourcefulness, and perseverance, though in a misguided cause. He is what Frodo would become, were he to surrender to the lure of the Ring. But since he is really a part of Frodo, he is not entirely evil, but only as evil as such a hero can be.

My son's young heart mourned Gollum's fall into the

fires of Mount Doom. So do the hearts of all who truly love this book.

With his two companions acting out the twin plots of growth and failure, Frodo is freed to follow a third path, one that is, though Tolkien labored hard to disguise the fact, essentially mystic. It begins with Frodo's wounding by the Nazgûl in the wood below Weathertop (this is the Fisher King's wound, and the reason he leaves no offspring behind), ennobles him through adversity, and reaches its climax in Mount Doom, when he dons the One Ring and claims its power for his own.

Of Frodo's inner journey, we know very little. Tolkien provided hints and mutters, and very little else, for the good and sufficient reason that he lacked the literary powers their explication would require. "That of which we cannot speak," as Wittgenstein put it, "we must pass over in silence." We know only that he suffers; and that his journey ultimately leads him to the Cracks of Doom.

The time of judgment is come at last. Frodo has failed the test. But no fair-minded person can believe he ever had a chance of passing it. Rather, he has been, as an engineer would put it, "tested to destruction." And, because he is judged for all his life rather than the weakness of an instant, he is spared from the damnation he has seemingly brought upon himself. Gollum, marked by all as a tool of Fate from the very beginning, steps in to save him.

Frodo is given mercy, rather than victory. This, too, marks the insight of age.

Mystics, however, cannot live in the real world. When the adventure is done, Frodo knows too much to ever find peace. He has leapfrogged over all his middle years, and carries the burden of age. There is no place left for him in all of Middle-earth save the Grey Havens . . . the Grey Havens and death. Sam follows Frodo partway on that journey, and then turns back. He sits down in a great chair before a roaring fire, his wife places his infant daughter on his knee, and he speaks the most heartbreaking line in all of modern fantasy:

"Well, I'm back," he said.

"No!" Sean cried, when I read those last words. I will bear the guilt of that forever. Reading, I was swept away by the words, by the momentum of the plot, and completely forgot about where they were heading, toward that terrible, beautiful eucatastrophic ending. I should have warned him it was coming. I should have prepared him for it. Possibly, I should even have lied and made up a different ending altogether, one in which "they all lived happily ever after."

But maybe not. What makes that moment hurt so much is how absolutely, undeniably *true* it is. It would be a mistake to tack a moral onto The Lord of the Rings as if it were merely a Brobdingnagian version of one of Aesop's fables. But Tolkien was writing about the world as he understood it, and in that world he had learned certain lessons: That pity is sometimes better than justice. That the best leaders are often filled with doubt. Most importantly, that life has consequences.

How could I deprive my son of the very point of the book?

Here is something that may sound terribly sentimental, but which nevertheless is absolutely true: I was present when my son was born. The midwife handed him first to his mother, and then, after a time, to me. He was placed in my arms. I looked down at that sweet little goblin face (he was born purple, for lack of oxygen, and only slowly turned pink). Someday, I thought, this child will grow up and become a man, and by so doing, turn me into an old man, and then I'll die. But that's all right. I don't mind. It's a small price to pay for him.

We live in a reflexively cynical age, and yet cynicism, though it encompasses a great deal of the truth, does not cover everything. That moment, looked at from the outside, comes perilously close to the saccharine. Yet, looked at as something experienced yourself, it is a glad and terrible thing to embrace the necessity of one's own death. It touches the soul like the first breath of autumn. It sounds a bell whose ultimate message is *goodbye*.

Such a moment requires books that can help us comprehend it.

As of this writing, my son is seventeen. In less than a year—about the time this essay reaches print—he will leave for college.

A young man is like a falcon. When you remove the hood and untie the jesses, he leaps from your arm and launches himself into the sky. You look at him dwindling, so proud and so free, and you wonder if he'll ever return to you.

IF YOU GIVE A GIRL A HOBBIT

ESTHER M. FRIESNER

I am a writer. I have received money for doing this on several occasions, so the odds are that I will continue on this unfortunate course until someone catches wise. (If you don't want a writer to come back, don't feed him. This is a good, practical rule, and applies to cats as well. Writers are a lot like cats in this and many other re-

spects, except for the part about being able to wash ourselves all over with our tongues. Dang.)

Having admitted to the crime of Authoring in the First
Degree, with Premeditation and Malice Aforethought, I
have no qualms about adding to my scroll of malfeasance
by saying that *what* I write is generally fantasy and science
fiction. This would be viewed as bad enough, in most re-
spectable venues (i.e., periodicals such as the *Pays-in-
Copies Review* or the *Deconstructionist Quarterly*), but I
have piled iniquity upon iniquity (which is easier than it
sounds, as long as you remember to lift with the legs, not
with the back): I have written *funny* fantasy and science
fiction. On purpose.

Up until now, I simply accepted this deep personal fail-
ing as something over which I had as little control as the
color of my eyes, the girth of my waistline, or the periodic
urge to shout "Macaroni!" in a crowded movie theater. Now
some well-meaning prats out there may argue that I *do so*
have the power to change any or all of the above. I can get
tinted contact lenses, I can chew less and eschew more;
and as for the whole "Macaroni!" thing, well, there is always
Pasta-avoidance Therapy (or a gig on Jerry Springer). They
claim that it is all a matter of giving it the Old School Try,
of getting off my duff and making a valiant effort, of striving
ever onward and upward for the night is coming. They may
be right. They may also be British.

But is that the answer I'm seeking? Do I want to learn
that I *can* control the unattractive, unhealthy, or socially
unacceptable portions of my life? Do I want to have the
golden door of Opportunity for Personal Improvement flung
wide by the same kindly hands that are equally ready to

frog-march me through same? Do I want to accept responsibility for my actions and the results thereof?

Of course I don't want that! It's too much like work. I'm an American. What I want is to keep on doing exactly what I've been doing all along, bad as it may be, only first I want to be told that it's okay because it is *not my fault*. Yes, what I need to find is *someone else to blame for it*.

I blame Tolkien.

(No, not for the "Macaroni!" *schtick*; for my having become a writer. Try to keep up with me here, okay?)

It all began back in the good old days, when a woman knew her place and the twin pillars upon which civilization rested were: *Everything will be all right as long as you have a matching set of china/silverware/crystal/linens/luggage* and *Real women don't read fantasy and/or science fiction; boys will think you're ooky*. (Of course, nowadays, the only person upholding the first of these principles is Martha Stewart, but since she *is* science fiction, I don't know where that leaves us as far as the second principle goes.)

Yes, it was a simpler time, and I was a simpler person. I believed with all the ardor of my teenaged heart that as long as I lived my life according to the tenets set forth within the hallowed pages of *Seventeen* magazine, I could not go wrong. (Although I did spend many a fruitless hour cudgeling my brains while trying to figure out what the heck all of those "Modess . . . Because" ads were selling. In case this phenomenon is before your time, in olden days it was considered indelicate to come right out and talk about, er, feminine hygiene products, even when you were trying to sell them. The ads in question always showed a woman dressed entirely in white, and placed in a romantic, usually moonlit setting, with the only text anywhere in the ad being: "Modess . . . Because." I kept yelling, "Because *what*?! Because *why*?! Dear Lord, tell me, else I shall run stark mad!" at the magazine until Mom made me stop. A friend of mind has since suggested that perhaps all the genteel societal taboos of our past surrounding girlstuff might seem less Neanderthal and more Empowering if we thought of them as contributing to the Women's Mysteries. "Agatha Christie . . . Because?" I don't *think* so.)

But I digress.

Then, one fateful day, it all changed. I was reading the new issue of *Seventeen,* and when I reached the book review column, what did my wondering-albeit-myopic eyes see but a paragraph in praise of something called *The Hobbit* by someone (O, vile enchanter!) named J. R. R. Tolkien.

They said it was a good book.

They said it was a fantasy, but they *still* said it was a good book.

They said it was a fantasy, and a good book, and that it would be all right if I actually went out and *read* it!

They implied that it would likewise be all right if I *admitted* to having read it afterward, even if I made said admission out in public where boys could hear me.

At first I was a bit suspicious. For all I knew, the person writing the book review column was some Machiavellian hag who had decided to give her helpless readers a bum steer because she didn't want us growing up to be her competition in the field of Matrimony. (Serve her right if we did grow up to snaffle up all the good husband material! That would teach the wizened crone to try having a career *and* marriage! The very notion!) Were I to read *The Hobbit* then somehow the boys would *know* that I had dabbled my frilly pink brain in the dark tarn of fantasy/science fiction and rendered it unattractive thereby. Since I was already wearing glasses, buying clothes in what they then referred to as the "Chub" department, and stuffing whole boxes of tissues into the cups of my Who-Do-You-Think-You're-Kidding training bra, I was not about to do anything else that might handicap me in the Great Husband Nab-a-thon that was life pre-Liberation.

And yet . . . and yet . . . and yet, this was *Seventeen* magazine, my guiding light, my girlie gospel, my glossy guardian angel through the sweltering, noxious, soul-devouring morass of adolescence. (Anyone who thinks I am exaggerating has not been a teenager for a *long* time.) If I couldn't trust it, well, what could I trust? Besides, the book did sound kind of . . . interesting. I went to the library and checked it out.

Shortly thereafter I was back at the library, clawing at the card catalog like a refugee from a Romero movie, only instead of "Braaaaiiins . . . Braaaaiiins . . ." I was moaning, "Tolkiiiieeeeeen . . . Tolkiiiieeeeeen . . ."

Which brings us to the trilogy. I can't blame Tolkien for my present writerly state without slopping a big, gooey ladleful of the onus onto the trilogy's platter.

I am not the first to blame things on the trilogy. Get any sizeable group of SF writers together and somewhere in it, like a hairball in a bowl of hummus, you will find one or more persons ready to tell you that Tolkien ruined it for everyone by inaugurating the Rule of Trilogies. Yes, according to some people, all post-Tolkien fantasy had to

THE BLACK RIDER

The Fellowship of the Ring

Chapter IV: "A Short Cut to Mushrooms"

come in three volumes or forget about it. (Of course, there is the little matter of Dante's *Divine Comedy,* which might likewise be viewed as the great-great-great-grandpappy of all fantasy trilogies, but don't bother bringing that up; no one's going to listen.)

Children, before we go on with this tale, let me remind you that all this took place in prehistoric times, before the Internet, before mega-malls, before the inexorable spread of the mammoth "chain" bookstores across the land. Why, in those days, if you wanted a cup of coffee, you could not walk to the corner Starbucks because there *was* no corner Starbucks, and all we had were woodburning corners that could only be reached uphill both ways in the snow! Dark times indeed.

Of course there *were* bookstores, just not in my neighborhood. This meant that when I wanted to get my grubby paws on the trilogy, I had no option but to check it out of the library. The trouble was, I wasn't the only one who wanted to read it. Someone else had checked out *The Fellowship of the Ring*, leaving the other two volumes behind.

I suppose I could have waited for *The Fellowship* to be returned. A rational person would have waited. But I was a woman possessed, for whom *patience* was just the name of a Gilbert & Sullivan operetta. I checked out *The Two Towers* and started reading the trilogy from the middle outward. I admit that this left me a little bewildered to start with. ("*Who* is this guy they're giving the Viking funeral for, and *how* did he die, and oh wow, is it just me or is that elf Legolas really *hot*?") But then, I'd had lots of practice being bewildered by all of those "Modess . . . Because" ads, so poor old Boromir's launch party was small potatoes as far as maximum total reader ferhoodlement went.

To make a long story short, I read the trilogy in two-three-one order, and came away from it a changed woman. The next thing I knew I was reading other fantasy novels. I no longer cared whether or not the boys found out about my shameful solitary vice. Who needs boys when you've got elves, man?! (Given that I was then attending an all-girls school, my chances of getting an honest-to-*Seventeen* date with a boy were about equal with the odds of being swept away to Galadriel's grove by someone tall, dark, and pointy-eared. And since the chances of finding a nice, *Jewish* elf were about what you'd expect, this was also the first time I even vaguely considered the possibility of falling for someone Different.)

The stage was set for the final degradation.

One evening, having declined Lord Ruthven's invitation to the ball, choosing instead to lounge about the family manor in my peignoir and bunny slippers, I turned on the television. There he was. Him. *My* him: Legolas the hottie elf. I could tell it was Legolas because he had pointy ears and, as everyone knows, all elves have pointy ears.

Previous to beholding *him* I had not realized that all elves likewise had pointy sideburns, puddingbowl hairstyles, upswept slanty eyebrows, and blue velour shirts, but I was willing to learn. By the time I finally came to comprehend that what I was watching/drooling over was not a televised version of the trilogy (William Shatner would not make a good hobbit in this or any other universe) it was too late: I'd become hooked on *Star Trek*. I was doomed.

You might think that once you are wallowing in the fantasy/science-fictional gutter there is nowhere lower for you to sink. Shows what you know, bucko.

Let us move the clock forward a tick or two, bringing us to my bright college years at Vassar. At that time, Vassar was not yet coeducational, so we are still talking about a heavy concentration of female hormones all dressed up and nowhere to go but the dorm TV room. We attended scheduled airtimes for *Star Trek* and *Dark Shadows* with a zealous regularity that left enclosed orders of Carmelite nuns looking like flibbertigibbets. But all of our merry schoolgirl crushes on emotionless Vulcans and haughty vampires did not mean we were averse to dating real men. (Though it *might* account for why so many of us went on to marry lawyers.)

I too wanted to date a real man, but wound up settling for a Yalie. He invited me to the prom; and while in lovely New Haven I discovered something that opened my eyes to a whole new world of primal, visceral, earth-shaking ecstacy: the Yale Co-op. When it comes to bookstores, size *does* matter.

It was here I bought the final nail in my coffin: *Bored of the Rings.* This was a parody of the trilogy produced by the *Harvard Lampoon* that was wonderful or sophomoric or both, according to the reader's taste. Since I *was* a sophomore at the time, I found it to be wonderful. From reading *Bored of the Rings* I learned that it was possible to take the adored icons and sacrosanct quest-plot and stick big red squeaky clown noses on anything that didn't get out of the way fast enough. (It's been my opinion that a good book can take a good joke and survive. Tolkien's work went the full ten rounds against *Bored of the Rings* and came back swinging. And even when they take a cream pie in the face, elves are *still* hot!)

I will draw a merciful veil over subsequent Tolkien-related incidents in my life, though some were educational. For example, when *everything* by Tolkien was flying off the shelves, publishers started trotting out *anything* by Tolkien, which might or might not have included his laundry lists. My apologies to Tolkien completists out there, but I never did appreciate *The Silmarillion*. Yet thus did I learn that if you become famous/profitable enough as a writer, *every last word* you ever penned in your lifetime will get trucked to market. (Note that "*you* ever penned in *your* lifetime" need not always apply, viz: V. C. Andrews.)

On the other hand, the Rankin-Bass animated production of *The Hobbit* and the Ralph Bakshi stab at Lord of the Rings were both . . . never mind. As with *Bored of the Rings,* we are in the realm of personal tastes, the ubiquitous YMMV of the Internet. Let's sidestep the flamewar and just change the subject.

So you see that I am fully within my rights when I refuse to accept responsibility for having become a writer of (often deliberately) funny fantasy and science fiction. It *is* all Tolkien's fault. His books were the gateway drug and yes, the first one *was* free. At his doorstep and no other must I abandon the following accusations:

1. Reading *The Hobbit* led me to read the three books of The Lord of the Rings. (And reading the books out of numerical order allowed me to understand that a good book is fully capable of standing alone even if it is one of a litter of three.)

2. Reading The Lord of the Rings led me to read other fantasy.

3. The Lord of the Rings—especially the Appendices—led me to realize that a good fantasy is one that springs from a fully realized world, and that constructing that world can be an awful lot of *fun*. When I wrote my first fantasy novel, if the characters did not all hail from one bland, uniform, all-encompassing Fairytale Culture, if they actually got a little frazzled and weary while on the road, if they remembered to pack a lunch—and other supplies—for the trip, and if they learned that even if you take down the Bad Guys, your world can never go back to being just the way it was before, all of the above was thanks to Tolkien.

   I know he's not the only one to have included those little details, but for me, he was the first.

4. The interesting characters in The Lord of the Rings (i.e. hottie elves) led me to watch *Star Trek*.

5. *Star Trek* led me to read science fiction as well as watch it.

6. Reading science fiction and fantasy led me into the James Fenimore Cooper trap. (J. F. C. was reading novels to his sick wife when he was reputed to have become fed up and exclaimed "Who *wrote* this muck? I could do better!" And he did, in his opinion, though definitely *not* in that of Mark Twain.) Yes, I became convinced that I could write no-pun-intended rings around some of the stuff that was actually getting published.

   Thus began the long, hard apprenticeship of

the pen (read: Hell) that brought me to my present low estate.

7. Reading Tolkien allowed me to understand what was so downright hilarious about *Bored of the Rings,* which in turn opened my eyes to the wide-open land of opportunity for writing *funny* fantasy and science fiction.

8. Writing per se led me to try writing with the avowed intention of getting money for it. This meant I would have to learn how to get money from *editors,* and if you think this is an easy task you are either armed with a crowbar, you are someone named Big Rocko, or you are armed with someone named Big Rocko. My first professional fiction sale was, in fact, a funny science-fiction story with a strong fantasy element ("The Stuff of Heroes," which appeared in the March 1983 issue of *Isaac Asimov's Science Fiction Magazine*), and that was it, the end of the road. I was lost beyond all hope of heaven to redeem.

But I got paid for it! And, having once tasted the fruits of victory (after I cashed the check and went out and bought some fruits, that is), I went back and did it again. And again. And again, and again, and *again,* and—!

So here I am and here I stay. Call me an ink-stained wretch or a pixel-packin' mama, but the underlying definition's the same: I am a writer, irrevocably seduced into the lush, steamy, torrid jungle of speculative fiction where even now I dwell, captive and content to be so. And whose fault is that, might I ask?

Tolkien's. None other. The culpability rests solely with him.

Well, him and those elves. Mm-*mmh*!

THE RING AND I

HARRY TURTLEDOVE

I discovered *The Hobbit* and The Lord of the Rings in summer 1966. I was seventeen; I had just graduated from high school, and was about to head off to the California Institute of Technology. I liked *The Hobbit* pretty well: well enough, at any rate, that I bought the trilogy to see what else J. R. R. Tolkien had written.

With The Lord of the Rings I was utterly entranced, and

have been from that day to this. What struck me most about the trilogy was the astonishing depth of Tolkien's creation. He had not simply imagined the fictional present in which his characters were living, but also a history thousands of years deep, as well as not one but several fictional languages. And what had happened in the dim and distant past of this created world kept bubbling up and remaining intensely relevant to the fictional present, in much the same way as Arminius the German's defeat of the Roman legions at the Teutoberg Wald in 9 A.D. remains intensely relevant to the history of Europe during the century.

I read *The Hobbit* and the trilogy obsessively. In the year after finding them, I must have gone through them, appendices and all, six or eight times. This was, of course, my freshman year at an academically demanding institution. Falling head over heels in love with The Lord of the Rings isn't the only reason I flunked out of Caltech. It isn't even the most important reason. But the time I spent with Frodo and Sam and Merry and Pippin was time I didn't spend—and should have spent—with physics and calculus and chemistry.

Nor was I the only one at Caltech caught up in Tolkien's spell. There were about ten of us, three or four, as luck would have it, in my residence house. We would get together when we could to try to stump one another with obscure quotations, to seek to work out the meanings of elvish words, and to argue about things as abstruse and unprovable as how well a Roman legion suddenly transported to the universe of The Lord of the Rings might fare: of this last, more anon.

We searched through the books for hints about how the

unwritten history of the Fourth Age might go as diligently as fifth-century theologians went over the New Testament for clues as to the nature or natures of Christ. I came to the conclusion that the chief evil power of the Fourth Age would be the Lord of the Nazgûl. This is, no doubt, heresy of the purest ray serene, but, like the Arians or Nestorians of early Christendom, I had some texts on my side.

Consider: The Fourth Age is to be the Age of Man, with the elves and other ancient races vanished or much reduced in power. The Nazgûl, proud men ensnared by Sauron's schemes, are the great bane of mankind. When Merry hamstrung the Lord of the Nazgûl, he did so with a blade from the Barrow-downs, a blade specially made with charms against Sauron's chief lieutenant, who had been the Witch-king of Angmar in the north. But when Owyn struck the blow that finished the Ringwraith, what sword did she use? Only an ordinary weapon of the Rohirrim. And when the Nazgûl's spirit left him, it "faded to a shrill wailing, passing with the wind, a voice bodiless and thin that died, and was swallowed up and was never heard again *in that age of the world* [italics mine]." Not in the Third Age, certainly. But what of the Fourth?

I may also note that, having thus been disembodied, the Lord of the Nazgûl was not caught, as were the other eight of his kind, in the incinerating eruption of Mount Doom after the Ring went into the fire. And, in a footnote to letter 246 in Carpenter's collection, Tolkien, who had been talking about how Frodo would have fared had he faced the remaining eight Nazgûl, writes, "The Witch-king [the Lord of the Nazgûl] had been reduced to impotence." Tolkien does not say the Ringwraith was slain, so I have, at least, a case.

Such was my reasoning. I should also note at this point that I was already trying to become a writer. I'd tried to write three different novels, and had actually finished one (none of this work, I hasten to add, came within miles of being publishable). The summer of 1967 was among the blackest times of my life. I had no idea how to cope with academic failure—thinking I could excel without studying much, as I had in high school, was a contributing factor, and not such a small one, to my flunking out of Caltech.

And so I plunged into a new novel. It was, of course, an exercise in hubris, complete and unadorned. I realize that now. I did not realize it when I was eighteen. There are a great many things one does not realize at eighteen, not least among them being how very many things one does not realize at eighteen. Taking some of the arguments from the Caltech dorms, my own growing interest in history, and my belief that the Lord of the Nazgûl survived, I dropped a couple of centuries of Caesar's legionaries (and one obstreperous Celt) into what I imagined Gondor would be like during the Fourth Age.

God help me, I still have the manuscript. The one thing I can truthfully say is that I meant no harm. (I take that back. I can say one other thing: I am not the individual mentioned in letter 292 of *The Letters of J. R. R. Tolkien,* the chap who not only aimed to write a sequel to The Lord of the Rings but sent Tolkien a detailed outline of it. That letter dates from December 1966, before part of the same bad idea occurred to me.)

I wrote it. I finished it: something close to 100,000

AMON HEN, THE SEAT OF SEEING

The Fellowship of the Ring

Chapter X: "The Breaking of the Fellowship"

words, far and away the longest project I'd ever undertaken up till then. Even had all the inspiration come from my own mind, I couldn't have sold it. Neither the style nor the characterization—such as that was—measures up to anything anyone else would ever want to read. To this day, though, I can say the plot was not disastrously bad. I had a tolerable story, but I didn't yet know how to tell it or where to set it.

A dozen years passed. I did a lot of the things most people do going from eighteen to thirty. I found something that interested me and pursued it. (In my case, it happened to be the history of the Byzantine Empire, which I admit is not a subject reckoned universally fascinating.) I fell in love several times. Sometimes this was mutual, sometimes not, which is also par for the course. Once, when it was, I got married. That lasted a little more than three and a half years. Not too long after my first wife and I broke up, I met the lady to whom I'm married now. In short, I grew up, or started to.

After I got my doctorate in Byzantine history, I taught for two years at UCLA while the professor under whom I'd studied had a guest appointment at the University of Athens. I had kept writing, and I began to sell an occasional piece: a science-fiction novelette to a magazine that expired before the piece saw print; a fantasy novel that owed nothing to Tolkien except, of course, a debt of gratitude for vastly broadening the market for fantasy novels of all sorts.

In the autumn of 1979, I was engaged to the woman now my wife, and unemployed—a combination always especially endearing to a prospective father-in-law—and hoping to find a job, any sort of job, before my savings ran out, and

I faced the ultimate indignity of my generation: having to move back into the house where I'd grown up. Being unemployed, I had time on my hands. I decided I would go to work on another fantasy novel. If all went extremely well, that would even help me pay my bills.

In pondering what to write, I remembered that novel I'd worked on in an earlier time of crisis, the one that dropped Romans from Caesar's legions into Fourth Age Gondor. By the time I reached thirty, I was smart enough to figure out that using someone else's universe—especially without his permission—was not the right way to go about things. I'd also spent all that time and effort acquiring specialized knowledge of my own. This time, I dropped the legionaries into a world of my own creation, rather than Tolkien's. I should have done that in the first place, but better late, I hoped, than never.

The world I built was modeled on the Byzantine Empire in the late eleventh century, at the time of the crucial battle of Manzikert, except that magic worked. Into it I brought my Romans—and one obstreperous Celt. The broad outlines of the plot of what became The Videssos Cycle are the same as those of my earlier act of unauthorized literary appropriation. This is why *The Misplaced Legion,* the first book of The Videssos Cycle, is dedicated to my wife, to the professor under whom I learned Byzantine history, to L. Sprague De Camp (whose *Lest Darkness Fall* first interested me in Byzantium) . . . and to J. R. R. Tolkien. My own cast of mind and my work usually resemble De Camp's far more than Tolkien's, but I felt I needed to note all the origins of the series. Attention must be paid.

Stretching and cutting the plot to fit the new situation

wasn't that hard. I had envisioned Gondor in the Fourth
Age as being in a situation the Byzantines would have understood: ancient; proud; diminished in territory from earlier days; in constant conflict with neighboring peoples,
some of them nomads off the plains. (To this day, that
seems reasonable to me. Tolkien himself, in letter 131 of
the Carpenter collection, writes, "In the south Gondor rises
to a peak of power, almost reflecting Númenór, and then
fades slowly to decayed Middle Age, a kind of proud, venerable, but increasingly impotent Byzantium." The analogy
was in his mind, too. The difference is, it had a right to be
in his, but not in mine, not in his universe.)

One problem I had with The Videssos Cycle was the
nature of my villain. The Lord of the Nazgûl was, as I mentioned, the chief evil power in my imagined Fourth Age.
When he appeared among men, he necessarily went veiled
and masked, as he had no face he could present to the
world. I incorporated this feature of his appearance into the
new world I was building: incorporated it without first asking myself, Why are you doing this?

By the time I did think to ask myself that question, my
masked and veiled villain had become an integral part of
the world I'd created. That meant I had to devise some
reason for his concealing himself, and one that needed to
be far removed from the reason the Nazgûl never showed
themselves. I hope I succeeded in this. Had I not transposed
quite so thoroughly from the Tolkien-based world to the
one I was creating myself, the difficulty never would have
arisen. And, indeed, it shouldn't have.

Aside from strip-mining my unpublishable homage to
The Lord of the Rings to help form work I might legitimately

show the world, I've used Tolkienesque motifs only once that springs to mind, in a short story called "After the Last Elf Is Dead." There, the borrowing was intentional and, I believe, necessary. Tolkien and many of his lesser imitators depict the struggle of Good and Evil, with Good triumphant, at some cost, in the end.

This is, of course, how we want the world to work. The question I looked at in "After the Last Elf Is Dead" is, what happens if it doesn't work that way? What does the world look like if Evil defeats Good? Turning common tropes on their ear is often one of the most enjoyable and thought-provoking things a writer can do.

One of the more profitable things a writer can do, however, is to repeat those tropes. Tolkien's influence on fantasy since the publication and enormous success of The Lord of the Rings has not been altogether beneficial. This is not his fault, I hasten to add. But he has had many imitators, and imitators of imitators, and imitators of imitators of imitators, until some heroic-quest fantasies resemble nothing so much as blurry sixth-generation photocopies of his great work, borrowing not only structure but bits of background such as noble, immortal elves, and wicked, bestial orcs as if they sprang from lore long in the public domain rather than from the imagination of a writer not yet thirty years dead!

One very successful imitator—at least in financial terms—stated quite openly in an interview that his method was to emulate all the elements of adventure in The Lord of the Rings and to suppress the mythological, theological, and linguistic themes: every bit of the lore and scholarship and depth that informed the original. I read his words in astonished disbelief and dismay. And yet, he proved a shrewd judge of what a substantial part of the reading public wanted, or was willing to settle for. His books outsell those of all but a handful of other writers in the field.

The essential difference, I think, is that Tolkien created his world for himself first, and for others only afterward. He began building the lays and legends of Middle-earth more than twenty years before even *The Hobbit* saw print. Almost twenty years more passed before The Lord of the Rings appeared. Everything in these books is a product of long reflection, long refinement. It shows. How could it help but show?

Because of that, it is unique, and is likely to remain so. Most books come into being far more quickly, and with at least one eye toward the market. It has always been so, ever since the earliest days of the printing press. Several of Shakespeare's plays, for instance, were first published as what we now call Bad Quartos—hasty, pirated editions designed to make a printer a fast buck. If we had only the Bad Quarto of *Hamlet*, the Prince of Denmark's immortal soliloquy would read:

> To be, or not to be. Ay, there's the point,
> To die, to sleep, is that all? Ay, all:
> No, to sleep, to dream, ay marry there it goes,
> For in that dream of death, when we awake,
> And borne before an everlasting Judge,
> From whence no passenger ever return'd,
> The undiscovered country, at whose sight
> The happy smile, and the accursed damn'd.
> But for this, the joyful hope of this,

> Who'd bear the scorns and flatteries of the world,
> Scorned by the right rich, the rich cursed of the
>   poor?

The difference between that sorry text—probably set in type relying on the shaky memory of one of the actors in the play—and what Shakespeare actually wrote is the same sort of gulf that lies between those who would imitate Tolkien and the man himself. It is the difference between haste and care, between commerce and love. (I don't mean to suggest that Tolkien was immune to concerns about commerce; any examination of his letters proves otherwise. But he had built his world long before commerce became a concern. It is not often, and cannot often be, thus.)

As I've noted before, perhaps the greatest debt of gratitude fantasists of all stripes—emphatically not just the imitators—owe to J. R. R. Tolkien is what his success did for the genre as a whole. A couple of generations ago, speaking in broad terms, fantasy was something writers occasionally turned out in between novels full of spaceships. Science fiction normally outsold it by a considerable margin.

It isn't like that any more. Fantasy novels, these days, appear on bestseller lists far more regularly than their counterparts from science fiction. And a rising tide lifts all boats. Fantasies that could not have hoped to find a home in the 1950s or 1960s now have a better chance of seeing print, because—in no small measure due too Tolkien's work—fantasy has become a recognized category of its own. It is no accident that the professional organization for those who produce speculative fiction recently changed its name from the Science Fiction Writers of America to the

Science Fiction and Fantasy Writers of America.

The next question to ask is, why has this happened? What has made Tolkien so enduringly popular? What has made fantasy in general so popular, besides Tolkien's example? Part of the answer, I think, lies in the ongoing, ever more rapid, changes in American life—indeed, in life throughout the industrialized world—during the course of the twentieth century, and especially after the end of World War II. We are all travelers nowadays. When we look back to our childhoods, we remember a world quite different from the one in which we live today.

Take me as an example. I am, as I write these words, fifty-one. Things we take for granted nowadays that either did not exist or were in their infancy when I was born include television; vaccines for polio, mumps, measles, and chicken pox (I had all but the first, though I didn't come down with chicken pox till the age of forty-three); frozen foods; jet airliners; no-fault divorce; most, though not all, antibiotics; audio- and videotapes; space travel and most of what we know of astronomy (in the 1950s, the canals of Mars and oceans of Venus were legitimate topics for hard science fiction); birth-control pills; microwave ovens; the civil rights, women's rights, gay rights, and environmental movements; freeways and the interstate highway system; rock 'n' roll; lasers; CDs; mass in the vernacular rather than Latin; computers; legal pornography; e-mail; the hydrogen bomb; organ transplants; and the World Wide Web. The list is brief, and far from comprehensive.

No wonder, then, that every so often we are tempted to stop and wonder, What the hell am I doing here? Throughout almost the entire course of human history, people lived in much the same world at the end of their lives as at the beginning. Change did happen, but incrementally, even glacially. Medieval artists dressed the Roman soldiers around the crucified Jesus in the armor of their own day, and saw nothing incongruous in doing so. That styles and techniques in such things had altered through time was beyond their mental horizon.

Only in the past couple of hundred years has change become rapid enough to grow visible in the course of a single human life. It is no accident that historical fiction—fiction emphasizing the differences between past and present—came into being at about the same time as the Industrial Revolution took flight. The smooth continuum between past and present was broken; the past became a separate country, and interesting specifically because of that.

I also think it no accident that fantasy has become so popular in an age of unprecedented change. It offers the reader a glimpse of a world where the verities underlying society endure, where moral values are strong (and, returning directly to Tolkien here, those who neglect the moral underpinnings of his work blind themselves to a large part of the world he built), where choices between Good and Evil are simpler than in the real world, and where Good may reasonably be expected to triumph in the end. It's an anchor on a wildly tossing sea. Sometimes, it can be a crutch.

Few of us, I think—I hope!—would care to live permanently in such a world. But, especially when presented as magnificently as Tolkien does, it is a wonderful place to visit. We can enjoy the intricate adventure for its own sake, and for the respite it gives us from the complications and frustrations of mundane life. And, perhaps, even after we set the books aside, we find ourselves a little more ready to face with good heart the world in which we do live. What more could one possibly ask of a work of the imagination?

CULT CLASSIC

TERRY PRATCHETT

The Lord of the Rings is a cult classic. I know that's
true, because I read it in the newspapers, saw it
on the TV, heard it on the radio.

We know what "cult" means. It's a put-down word. It
means "inexplicably popular but unworthy." It's a word
used by the guardians of the one true flame to dismiss anything that is liked by the wrong kind of people. It also means

"small, hermetic, impenetrable to outsiders." It has associations with cool drinks in Jonestown.

The Lord of the Rings has well over one hundred million readers. How big will it have to be to emerge from cult status? Or, once having been a cult—that is to say, once having borne the mark of Cain—is it actually possible that anything can *ever* be allowed to become a full-fledged Classic?

But democracy has been in action over the past few years. A British bookshop chain held a vote to find the country's favorite book. It was The Lord of the Rings. Another one not long afterward, held this time to find the favorite author, came up with J. R. R. Tolkien.

The critics carped, which was expected but nevertheless strange. After all, the bookshops were merely using the word "favorite." That's a very personal word. No one ever said it was a synonym for "best." But a critic's chorus hailed the results as a terrible indictment on the taste of the British public, who'd been given the precious gift of democracy and were wasting it on quite unsuitable choices. There were hints of a conspiracy amongst the furry-footed fans. But there was another message, too. It ran: "Look, we've been trying to tell you for *years* which books are good! And you just don't *listen*! You're not listening now! You're just going out there and buying this damn book! And the worst part is that we can't stop you! We can tell you it's rubbish, it's not relevant, it's the worst kind of escapism, it was written by an author who never came to our parties and didn't care what we thought, but unfortunately the law allows you to go on not listening! You are stupid, stupid, *stupid!*"

And, once again, no one listened. Instead, a couple of

years later, a national newspaper's Millennium Masterworks poll produced five works of what could loosely be
called "narrative fiction" among the top fifty "masterworks" of the last thousand years, and, yes, there was The
Lord of the Rings *again*.

The Mona Lisa was also in the top fifty masterworks. And
I admit to suspecting that she was included by many of the
voters out of a sheer cultural knee-jerk reaction, mildly dis-
honest but well meant. Quick, quick, name of the greatest
works of art of the last thousand years! Er . . . er . . . well,
the Mona Lisa, obviously. Fine, fine, and have you *seen* the
Mona Lisa? Did you stand in front of her? Did the smile
entrance you, did the eyes follow you around the room and
back to your hotel? Er . . . no, not as such . . . but, uh, well,
it's the Mona Lisa, okay? You've *got* to include the Mona
Lisa. And that guy with the fig leaf, yeah. And that woman
with no arms.

That's honesty, of a sort. It's a vote for the good taste of
your fellow citizens and your ancestors as well. Joe Average
knows that a vote for a picture of dogs playing poker is
probably not, when considered against the background of
one thousand years, a very sensible thing to cast.

But The Lord of the Rings, I suspect, got included when
people stopped voting on behalf of their culture and quietly
voted for what they liked. We can't all stand in front of one
picture and feel it open up new pathways in our brain, but
we can—most of us—read a mass-market book.

I can't remember where I was when JFK was shot, but I
can remember exactly where and when I was when I first
read J. R. R. Tolkien. It was New Year's Eve, 1961. I was
babysitting for friends of my parents while they all went out

to a party. I didn't mind. I'd got this three-volume yacht anchor of a book from the library that day. Boys at school had told me about it. It had maps in it, they said. This struck me at the time as a pretty good indicator of quality.

I'd waited quite a long time for this moment. I was that kind of kid, even then.

What can I remember? I can remember the vision of beech woods in the Shire; I was a country boy, and the hobbits were walking through a landscape which, give or take the odd housing development, was pretty much the one I'd grown up in. I remember it like a movie. There I was, sitting on this rather chilly sixties-style couch in this rather bare room; but at the edges of the carpet, the forest began. I remember the light as green, coming through trees. I have never since then so truly had the experience of being inside the story.

I can remember the click of the central heating going off and the room growing colder, but these things were happening on the horizon of my senses and weren't relevant. I can't remember going home with my parents, but I do remember sitting up in bed until 3:00 A.M., still reading. I don't recall going to sleep. I *do* remember waking up with the book open on my chest, and finding my place, and going on reading. It took me, oh, about twenty-three hours to get to the end.

Then I picked up the first book and started again. I spent a long time looking at the runes.

Already, as I admit this, I can feel the circle of new, anxious but friendly faces around me: "My name is Terry and I used to draw dwarf runes in my school notebooks. It started with, you know, the straight ones, everyone can do them, but then I got in deeper and before I knew it I was doing the curly elf ones with the dots. Wait . . . there's worse. Before I'd even heard the word 'fandom' I was writing weird fan fiction. I wrote a crossover story setting Jane Austen's *Pride and Prejudice* in Middle-earth; the rest of the kids loved it, because a class of thirteen-year-old boys with volcanic acne and groinal longings is not best placed to appreciate Miss Austen's fine prose. It was a really good bit when the orcs attacked the rectory. . . ." But around about then, I suspect, the support group would have thrown me out.

Enthralled I was. To the library I went back, and spake thusly: "Have you got any more books like these? Maybe with maps in? And runes?"

The librarian gave me a mildly disapproving look, but I ended up with *Beowulf* and a volume of Norse sagas. He meant well, but it wasn't the same. It took someone several stanzas just to say who they were.

But that drew me to the Mythology shelves. The Mythology shelves were next to the Ancient History shelves. What the hell . . . it was all guys with helmets, wasn't it? On, on . . . maybe there's a magical ring! Or runes!

The desperate search for the Tolkien effect opened up a new world for me, and it was this one.

History as it was then taught in British schools was big on kings and acts of Parliament, and was full of dead people. It had a certain strange, mechanistic structure to it. What happened in 1066? The Battle of Hastings. Full marks. And what else happened in 1066? What do you mean, what else happened? The Battle of Hastings was what 1066 was *for*. We'd "done" the Romans (they came, they saw, they had some baths, they built some roads and left) but my private reading colored in the picture. We hadn't "done" the Greeks. As for the empires of Africa and Asia, did *anyone* "do" them at all? But hey, look here in this book; these guys don't use runes, it's all pictures of birds and snakes; but, look, they know how to pull a dead king's brains out through his nose. . . .

And on I went, getting the best kind of education possible, which is the one that happens while you think you're having fun. Would it have happened anyway? Possibly. We never know where the triggers are. But The Lord of the Rings was a step-change in my reading. I was already enjoying, but The Lord of the Rings opened me up to the rest of the library.

I used to read it once a year, in the spring.

I've realized that I don't any more, and I wonder why. It's not the dense and sometime ponderous language. It's not because the scenery has more character than the characters, or the lack of parts for women, or the other perceived or real offenses against the current social codes.

It's simply because I have the movie in my head, and it's been there for forty years. I can still remember the luminous green of the beechwoods, the freezing air of the mountains, the terrifying darkness of the dwarf mines, the greenery on the slopes of Ithilien, west of Mordor, still holding out against the encroaching shadow. The protagonists don't figure much in the movie, because they were never more to me than figures in a landscape that was, itself, the hero. I remember it at least as clearly as—no, come to think of it, *more* clearly than—I do many of the places I've visited in what we like to call the real world. In fact, it is strange

GALADRIEL

The Fellowship of the Ring

Chapter VII: "The Mirror of Galadriel"

to write this and realize that I can remember stretches of the Middle-earth landscape as real places. The characters are faceless, mere points in space from which their dialogue originated. But Middle-earth is a place I went to.

I suppose the journey was a form of escapism. That was a terrible crime at my school. It's a terrible crime in a prison; at least, it's a terrible crime to a jailer. In the early sixties, the word had no positive meanings. But you can escape *to* as well as *from*. In my case, the escape was a truly Tolkien experience, as recorded in his *Tree and Leaf*. I started with a book, and that led me to a library, and that led me everywhere.

Do I still think, as I did then, that Tolkien was the greatest writer in the world? In the strict sense, no. You can think that at thirteen. If you still think it at fifty-three, something has gone wrong with your life. But sometimes things all come together at the right time in the right place—book, author, style, subject and reader. The moment was magic.

And I went on reading; and, since if you read enough books you overflow, I eventually became a writer.

One day I was doing a signing in a London bookshop and next in the queue was a lady in what, back in the eighties, was called a "power suit" despite its laughable lack of titanium armor and proton guns.

She handed over a book for signature. I asked her what her name was. She mumbled something. I asked again . . . after all, it was a noisy bookshop. There was another mumble, which I could not quite decipher. As I opened my mouth for the third attempt, she said, "It's Galadriel, okay?"

I said: "Were you by any chance born in a cannabis plantation in Wales?" She smiled, grimly. "It was a camper van in Cornwall," she said, "but you've got the right idea."

It wasn't Tolkien's fault, but let us remember in fellowship and sympathy all the Bilboes out there.

A BAR AND A QUEST

ROBIN HOBB

J can't write a scholarly essay about Tolkien. I'm not
a scholar. Nor can I produce a carefully reasoned
analysis of just how The Lord of the Rings changed not only
fantasy but literature for my generation and generations to
come. I am not only too close to it, I am at ground zero. I
am a product of his impact. Like the rider in the rocket, I
don't know the mechanics of launching it or the thought

that went into designing it. All I can tell you is that it carried me up to where I could see the stars, and nothing has looked quite the same since.

1965? I think that is right. Odd that I cannot put a more precise date to it. My family lived in a log house in a rural setting outside Fairbanks, Alaska. So I was about thirteen.

In the front yard of our log house, on stilt legs about fourteen feet tall, there was a small log cabin. In the dark cold of an Alaskan winter, in a good year, that cache was full of meat. Quarters of moose or caribou, frozen solid, leaned hooves-up against the walls. The hide was left on this grisly plenty to protect the meat from drying out. We had an electric freezer on the back porch as well, but the cache provided a space to store our hunting bounty until it could be cut into serving portions, wrapped in white paper and set into the plug-in freezer (which, often enough in the Fairbanks cold, was not plugged in for most of the winter!).

In summer, the cache served an entirely different purpose. It was mine. In a household rampant with seven siblings, not to mention their friends hanging out, it provided a small space of privacy for me. Bedrooms and living room had to be shared. No one except me wanted the cache. I could drag sleeping bags and cushions up there, and, for the summer at least, have my own room. With me went my books. Lots of books. Out of sight of both parents and siblings, I could hide from chores and the world at large, and read. One of the untrumpeted benefits of that Midnight Sun is that a flashlight is not necessary for late-night summer-reading. With plenty of Off! insect repellent and army-surplus mummy bag, my evening was complete.

This was the setting for not only my first reading of The

Lord of the Rings, but for many repetitions of it. The sensory memories connected with those books are bumpy cottonwood logs under my back and glimpses of blue sky through the close-set logs of the cache's roof.

I started with the Houghton Mifflin paperback with the pinky cover for *The Hobbit,* brought home from the rack at the drugstore. I went on to the Ace rip-offs for The Lord of the Rings. When I discovered that those who were courteous at least to living authors would not have bought the Ace editions, I saved rigorously and purchased all four books in Houghton Mifflin hardbacks. They cost me a whopping $5.95 each. It took me so long to acquire the whole set that the bindings did not match.

The Hobbit had, of course, Tolkien's own art on the cover. Two had jackets by Walter Lorraine, and the third had the darker art by Robert Quackenbush. But the covers didn't much matter to me. It was the pages within that I needed to possess. The same hardback editions still sit on the shelves in my office. Their dust jackets are frayed and eroded. Opened, they lie flat, the stitching peeking out at me between the pages. Yet, opened to any page, the words still have the power to draw me in and pull me under, and, ultimately, to take me home.

I have lost track of how many times I have reread them over the years. Nor can I recall how many copies of The Lord of the Rings I have purchased over the years. They have been gifts for friends, both young and old; and there have been sets that went off to college with my children. The last time I reread *The Hobbit* was less than a month ago, as I shared it with my youngest daughter. I can recite the opening paragraph from memory, yet I never deliberately memorized it. Phrases and sensory images from the books float up into my mind at odd times: "fireweed seeding away into fluffy ashes," winter apples that were "withered but sound," or the smell of fresh mushrooms rising from a covered basket.

I suspect it is difficult for readers who have grown up in a time when *The Hobbit* and The Lord of the Rings are acknowledged as classics to understand the breathtaking impact they had on readers like myself. I simply had never read anything like it. I was an omnivorous reader, steeped in fairy tale books, the classics, mythology, mysteries, and adventure. In those days before I discovered Tolkien, I was devouring science fiction and pulp at the junkie rate of at least a paperback a day. It wasn't that there was no good stuff out there. There was. I'd found Heinlein and Bradbury and Simak and Sturgeon and Leiber. All those encounters marked me. But Tolkien claimed me as no other writer ever had before.

His magic wrapped me and took me under, and when I came out of it, I was a different creature. Even as I sit here now, looking at a computer screen and trying to analyze why that is so, I am somewhat at a loss to explain it. Maybe it was the age I was, or the place I was in my development of reading taste. Maybe it was just the juxtaposition of Tolkien's Middle-earth and the restless sixties. But perhaps magic doesn't have to offer any explanation for why it worked. Perhaps it simply is.

Yet I think I can sieve out a bit of it. I had three distinct sensations at the end of The Lord of the Rings. One was the simple, unbelievable void of "It's over. There's no more of it to read." The second was, "And I've never encountered

anything like this. I'll never find anything this good again."
The third was perhaps the most alarming: "In all my life, I
will never write anything as good as this. He's done it; he's
achieved it. Is there any point in my trying?"

Taking the third sensation first: Even in those days, I
knew I was going to be a writer. I had been writing since I
was in first grade, creating short stories almost as soon as
I mastered sentences. By the time I finished junior high, I
burned with the fixed ambition that I was going to write
amazing books, someday. To discover that someone had
already written the most amazing books that could possibly
exist raised the bar to an almost impossible height for me.

Raising that bar was the most wonderful thing that anyone could have done for an ambitious young writer.

The fantasy I had read before that time simply didn't
take itself seriously. Before anyone sends me a list of a hundred serious fantasy books that existed before Tolkien
wrote, let me concede that I completely accept all responsibility for my ignorance. I am sure there was important
fantasy out there, and some of it had probably even made
it to Fairbanks, Alaska. I'm simply saying that I hadn't
found it. Not until The Lord of the Rings.

Much of the fantasy I had read before Tolkien was un-
mistakably written "for children." Some of it had that
snide, winking-at-the-grown-up-in-the-room humor that
some adults find amusing and children find irritating. (After
all, if you think I'm that stupid, why are you writing for
me?) Some was written with the kind of humor that becomes a barrier to the reader taking the character or story
seriously. How can you care about the hero when his next
contrived pratfall is probably less than a page away? Why

commit to a character whom the writer has not invested in emotionally?

Much of what I read was sword-and-sorcery, rollicking adventurous stuff; fun, but written with a fine disregard for any morality regarding theft or mercenary murder. Serious, long-term relationships among the characters did not seem to exist. The happy ending was usually that the character managed to walk away unscathed and unchanged. Some of the fantasy I'd read was written in the simplistic "Once upon a time" format where the Prince and the Giant and the Glass Mountain are all capitalized, just to make sure the reader knows he is in the throes of a classic fairy tale. Even *The Hobbit,* much as I enjoyed it, was not devoid of some such condescension toward its characters.

Yet in *The Hobbit* I discovered elements that had never before shone so clearly for me. Setting was fully developed. True setting is far more than descriptive passages about birch trees in winter, or picturesque villages. Tolkien's setting invoked a time and a place that was as familiar as home to me, yet unfolded the wonders and dangers of all that I had always suspected was just beyond the next hill. Here, too, were characters that rang as true as chimes, pompous Thorin and competent Balin, and Gandalf the wizard, subtle and quick to anger. I met them, and as the book progressed, I knew them. Tolkien allowed me to love them, without fear that on the next page I would discover the hollow cardboard or the contortion in the plot for the sake of a pun. Nor was the plot a linear thing, however the "There and Back Again" on the title page might imply it. It sprawled out in odd directions, touching older magics with the calm assumption that the reader would know they had

RIVENDELL

The Fellowship of the Ring

Book 2, Chapter I: "Many Meetings"

always existed and always would. Magic rings and Mirk-
wood were not issues that could be neatly cookie-cuttered
to fit within the covers of this book. They extended beyond
the edges of the page, and Tolkien made no apology for that.
Like the maps in the hardbacks, his word unfolded larger
than mere covers could encompass.

But more challenging to me was that this writer wrote
about things that mattered, and he did not scruple to say
so. If you take what someone else has stolen, can it ever be
truly yours? What matters more, loyalty to your friends or
preventing widespread bloodshed? There were issues of
what comprised real courage, and when did doing what was
right become more important than doing what was glorious.
Bilbo was a simple character, good-hearted and honest, yet
complex in that he faced decisions where happily ever after
extended beyond a question of personal gain or safety.

The ending was not what I had expected. Surely Bilbo
had deserved to be the flamboyant hero, the slayer of the
dragon? And the dwarves! I had expected Thorin to indeed
finish as King Under the Mountain, with all the dragon's
gold, and his companions all intact. What had become of
the requisite Happily Ever After, in which everything fin-
ishes exactly as it was at the beginning of the story, only
better?

Clearly, this writer who had chummed me in with a
"once upon a time" beginning was up to something.

I picked up *The Fellowship of the Ring* with the impression that I now knew what to expect of Tolkien. I was
wrong. Almost at once, I was swept from the deceptively
ordinary birthday party preparations into the darkness and
intrigue of ancient magic. A subtle change in both language

and tone gave fair warning that I had stepped past the interface of "fairy tale" into the darkness and intrigue of ancient magic. Issues I thought had been resolved in *The Hobbit* were revealed as but the tip of the iceberg. Even characters I thought I knew suddenly showed a greater depth of being.

Gandalf was more than an irascible wizard; he was a force moving in this world, a power to be reckoned with. Bilbo's indecisiveness about the Ring troubled me. If Tolkien had not already convinced me to care deeply about that character, that dilemma would not have been such a harbinger of things to come.

Tolkien had warned me that one could step out into the road and simply be swept away by it, carried off to parts not only unknown, but unimagined. His words took me, and for three volumes, spanning six books, I was his. I had read long books before. I had read series of books about the same characters. But (and this may seem inconceivable to current fantasy readers) this was my first encounter with a trilogy, a single story told in three volumes. Never before had I read one work that spanned so many pages. The impact was much greater than, "Wow, this is really a long story." To my way of thinking, the story and my experience of it were all too brief. Tolkein had been allowed the pages and the sheer number of words required to flesh out this world. I had experienced the depth that fantasy could have. For years afterward, other fantasy books, no matter how profound, would seem shallow in comparison. I would hunger for the richness of prose that took its time to tell the story, not as efficiently as possible, but as intricately as the tale deserved.

So that was the gauntlet that had been thrown down before me as a potential writer. Could I do what he had done? Could I create fantasy that had a moving, intricate plot, a rich setting, and characters that stepped off the page and into the reader's heart? The bar had been raised.

And knowing instinctively that the bar had been raised, my first two sensations were all the more disheartening. I'd finished reading The Lord of the Rings, and there was no more of it to devour. And I feared I'd never again find anything that would satisfy me as it had.

A bit of digression: I was not alone in this reaction. The most common comments I've heard from readers of my generation who were likewise thunderstruck by Tolkien's Lord of the Rings are that they had never read anything like it, and that they immediately tried to find more books like it. Some even immediately sat down and tried to write books "just like that" in the hopes of satisfying their own hunger for more. So, in a sense, he sent a whole generation of us forth on a quest. We were doomed to fail, of course. There was not, and simply is not, anything that is "just like" The Lord of the Rings. But because I didn't know that, I and others like me plunged into the search wholeheartedly. Like many a quest for the magnificently elusive, the ultimate significance was not that I didn't find my grail, but that I went forth, wholeheartedly seeking.

Of course, I read Tolkien's "lesser" works: *Farmer Giles of Ham* and *The Adventures of Tom Bombadil, Tree and Leaf,* and *Smith of Wooton Major*. I researched the works that Tolkien said had inspired him: *Sir Gawain and the Green Knight*. Icelandic Sagas. I was suddenly mining whole new sections of the public library. I had been a voracious and indiscriminate reader all my life. English teachers had sought in vain to instill in me some appreciation for "literature." Required reading lists and formulaic book report requirements hadn't done it. But with one shot, J. R. R. Tolkien had injected it straight into my heart. I think that by stepping back, past the recent layer of American literature, even past what I had been introduced to as English literature, I suddenly came to a place where I was connecting with Story itself. Stripped of setting and literary devices that had become too familiar to me, I suddenly came to traces of the raw essence that had powered Tolkien's work.

Earlier, I mentioned that I feel I read Tolkien at precisely the right time in my life. Prior to that time, he would have touched me, but not as deeply. I would not have been ready to hear him. Later, I might perhaps have been too jaded and disaffected to take the stories into my heart. But he struck a chord with me, and sent me on my quest. I carried his stories with me into high school, a difficult four years for me, where they were both my armor and my retreat.

I began to encounter other Tolkien readers who had also claimed the books as their own. I recall a birthday tea held one September 22 in honor of Bilbo's birthday. The school, somewhat puzzled, allowed us to use the nurse's room, for no other space was free for us. (We certainly could not be allowed to take tea into the library!) It was attended by two other Tolkein aficionados, the school librarian and myself. It was a self-congratulatory in-group of people who had discovered the finest of literature. I did not know any of the other attendees well, and yet it was very easy to acknowledge that a strong bond existed nonetheless.

In college, I encountered a different phenomenon. I was sent "outside" for college, off to Denver University in the "lower forty-eight." Culture shock was pretty jolting for this Alaskan kid. The smog made my eyelashes fall out. The dining-hall diet, bereft of moose and caribou, and with what seemed to me only a modicum of red meat, left me anemic. But most shocking of all were those people who seemed to think that Tolkien and The Lord of the Rings belonged to them. Foolish mortals. I knew it was mine, all mine, in a way they could never even comprehend. A girl who insisted her friends should call her Galadriel, and a short young man who tried to convince himself and others that he was likely part-hobbit, appalled me. Were they out of their minds? It was literary sacrilege.

You could not enter Tolkien's world that way, smearing its glory onto yourself and attempting to take it over. The only possible entry was to come into it as reader, as honored guest. The words were to be experienced as Story, not tried on like ill-fitting Halloween costumes. The depth of offense I felt still comes back to me after all those years. It was not, I told myself, at all the same as the way I signed notes to myself as Smeagol. Even if my more-knowing friends occassionally referred to me by that name, I knew I was not Smeagol. Smeagol was simply one of the keys, a character that opened the story to me. I would never think of dressing as Smeagol or publicly proclaiming that I truly was Smeagol.

It is strange to think that, in some ways, my love of Tolkien's Lord of the Rings became a barrier. I couldn't talk about Tolkien to those people, any more than I could discuss his work with those benighted fools who insisted that it was all symbolism, that Frodo was Christ sacrificed by Bilbo the Father. Refused to be distracted by such ridiculous notions. I knew I had to keep my focus. The Lord of the Rings was The Lord of the Rings, not a pattern for my life or an alternate religion.

I had to understand it as Story.

All through those years, and throughout my college experiences, my quest continued. Like a gold-panner, following that elusive trace of "color" up-stream, I sifted my reading for the bits and pieces of pure element, looking for the mother lode of Story. I don't know when it happened, but after a time the object of my quest shifted and became, not to find something "just like" Tolkien, but to tap the sources from which this magical work had come.

It is a quest that continues for me, up to this very day and hour. In the thirty-odd years of that seeking, I've slowly come to discover that the shards of Story that I am looking for are not necessarily buried in the literature of the distant past, or even on the shelves of libraries. With my painstakingly assembled templates, I can now discern those elements in any number of disparate places. I've collected pieces from the old fairy tales that were always so dear to me, and heard the clear ringing of Story in the bragging tales told in sailor bars.

Even more thrilling to me is when I pick up a new book by one of my contemporaries and discover that someone else not only has succeeded at tapping that ultimate Story source, but has deployed it with the trifold foundation of solid plot, detailed setting, and genuine characters. Almost without exception, I discover that I have just encountered someone who, like myself, embarked on a quest after reading Tolkien. The quest has borne fruit for me, not in that I ever found anything "just like" Tolkien but that I had his works as a touchstone to help me distinguish True Story from the Verbiage of the Week.

In the long years since I first hid in a meat cache and journeyed all through Middle-earth, I've heard a great deal of criticism of Tolkien. That he has "no strong female characters," that the books move too slowly, that he does not tell us enough about what the characters are feeling and thinking are perhaps the most common complaints. Some of this strikes me, quite frankly, as the criticism of those who want writers of a different time and place to miraculously conform to what is considered politically correct now. Some strike me as a complaint of readers wishing that all writers wrote in what we consider to be a "simple, modern style." I continue to be astonished by people who tell me that they couldn't get past the third chapter, or that they were bored, or could find no character to identify with. Sometimes I am left wondering if we have read the same books at all. But perhaps in the end it all comes down to discovering his magic at the right place and time in your own life. If that is so, then all I can say is that I am grateful that I was the recipient of that miraculous coincidence of time and situation.

He has left his mark on me. Even after all the years, the bar he raised for my writing is still as high. I am still striving to leap it as effortlessly and cleanly as he did. I still come away with bruised shins, but the drive to attempt it has not diminished. Likewise, I continue to quest for Story, though these days I accept that I will never find anything "exactly like" J. R. R. Tolkien's Lord of the Rings. The only possible fix for that hunger is to pick up those worn hardbacks again and once more enter into a world that has perhaps become more familiar but no less wondrous to me over the years.

And as I wonder whether I have said all I want to say here, the perfect coincidence occurs. It is one of those deus ex machina happenings that good editors throw out and life throws at us near constantly. A sharp hammering at the door downstairs interrupts my quiet morning with my computer and my cup of coffee. No sign of dwarves nor wizards with staffs denting my front door, but only the UPS man who has thoughtfully left a package just far enough away from the threshold that I have to go out barefoot on the frozen porch to claim it.

I don't hesitate. Stenciled down the side of it is "TITLE: J. R. R. Tolkien." It has come from overseas. I drag it in and haul it upstairs to my office before tearing into it. Treasures long awaited come to light. HarperCollins hardbacks with the Alan Lee illustrations; *The Hobbit* and a delicious fat single hardback containing The Lord of the Rings in one volume with gleaming dust jackets in a sturdy box. Slit the wrap with a thumbnail and pull them out to heft the books. I open one, testing the sturdiness of the binding. Ah. A good print size. I lean closer and smell the delicious scent of new book. Well, these should get me through another thirty years. What else? A paperback of *Farmer Giles of Ham*, embellished exactly as it should be with Pauline Bayne's art. And at the bottom a boxed edition of *The Hobbit*, in a very portable size, including postcards with Tolkien's art and an unfolding map with images by John Howe. It also includes a CD of Tolkien reading from his work, which could become a supplement to my well-preserved LP of him reading Elvish. I think I intended this last one as a Christmas gift for someone, but at the moment I can't recall for whom, and the CD is already playing. The familiar rich voice fills my office, and suddenly Gollum is "looking out of his pale lamp-like eyes" as he paddles his little boat on the underground lake. Too late. This is mine, My Precious, and I doubt it will ever be gift-wrapped and placed under a tree.

I open the handy little edition of *The Hobbit* and thumb through it. Hmm. They have appended the first chapter of *The Fellowship of the Ring* to the end, as a teaser. I am not sure I approve. Yet there, on the last page of the book, like a benediction, is a promise for me. Gandalf speaks to me: "Good-bye now! Take care of yourself! Look out for me, especially at unlikely times!"

Indeed. I think I always shall.

RHYTHMIC PATTERN IN THE LORD OF THE RINGS

URSULA K. LE GUIN

Since I had three children, I've read Tolkien's trilogy aloud three times. It's a wonderful book to read aloud or (consensus by the children) listen to. Even when the sentences are long, their flow is perfectly clear, and follows the breath; punctuation comes just where you need to pause; the cadences are graceful and inevitable. Like Charles Dickens and Virginia Woolf, Tolkien must have heard what he wrote. The narrative prose of such nov-elists is like poetry in that it wants the living voice to speak it, to find its full beauty and power, its subtle music, its rhythmic vitality.

Woolf's vigorous, highly characteristic sentence-rhythms are purely and exclusively prose: I don't think she ever uses a regular beat. Dickens and Tolkien both occasionally drop into metrics. Dickens's prose in moments of high emotional intensity tends to become iambic, and can even be scanned: "It is a far, far better thing that I do/than I have ever done . . ." The hoity-toity may sneer, but this iambic beat is tremendously effective—particularly when the metric regularity goes unnoticed as such. If Dickens recognized it, it didn't bother him. Like most really great artists, he'd use any trick that worked.

Woolf and Dickens wrote no poetry. Tolkien wrote a great deal, mostly narratives and "lays," often in forms taken from the subjects of his scholarly interest. His verse often shows extraordinary intricacy of meter, alliteration, and rhyme, yet is easy and fluent, sometimes excessively so. His prose narratives are frequently interspersed with poems, and once at least in the trilogy he quietly slips from prose into verse without signaling it typographically. Tom Bombadil, in *The Fellowship of the Ring,* speaks metrically. His name is a drumbeat, and his meter is made up of free, galloping dactyls and trochees, with tremendous forward impetus: Tum tata Tum tata, Tum ta Tum ta. . . . "You let them out again, Old Man Willow! What be you a-thinking of? You should not be waking. Eat earth! Dig deep! Drink water! Go to sleep! Bombadil is talking!" Usually Tom's speech is printed without line breaks, so unwary or careless silent readers may miss the beat until they *see* it as verse— as song, actually, for when his speech is printed as verse Tom is singing.

As Tom is a cheerfully archetypal fellow, profoundly in touch with, indeed representing, the great, natural rhythms of day and night, season, growth and death, it's appropriate that he should talk in rhythm, that his speech should sing itself. And, rather charmingly, it's an infectious beat; it echoes in Goldberry's speech, and Frodo picks it up. "Goldberry!" he cries as they are leaving, "My fair lady, clad all in silver green! We have never said farewell to her, nor seen her since that evening!"

If there are other metric passages in the trilogy, I've missed them. The speech of the elves and noble folk such as Aragorn has a dignified, often stately gait, but not a regular stress beat. I suspected King Théoden of iambics, but he only drops into them occasionally, as all measured English speech does. The narrative moves in balanced cadences in passages of epic action, with a majestic sweep reminiscent of epic poetry, but it remains pure prose. Tolkien's ear was too good and too highly trained in prosody to let him drop into meter unknowingly.

Stress units—metric feet—are the smallest elements of rhythm in literature, and in prose probably the only quantifiable ones. A while ago I got interested in the ratio of stresses to syllables in prose, and did some counting.

In poetry, the normal ratio is about 50 percent: that is, by and large, in poetry, one syllable out of two has a beat on it: Tum ta Tum ta ta Tum Tum ta, etc. . . . In narrative, that ratio goes down to one beat in two to four: ta Tum tatty Tum ta Tum tatatty, etc. . . . In discursive and technical writing, only every fourth or fifth syllable may get a beat; textbook prose tends to hobble along clogged by a superfluity of egregiously unnecessary and understressed polysyllables.

Tolkien's prose runs to the normal narrative ratio of one stress every two to four syllables. In passages of intense action and feeling the ratio gets pretty close to 50 percent, like poetry; but only Tom's speech can be scanned.

Stress beat in prose is fairly easy to identify and count, though I doubt any two readers of a prose passage would mark the stresses in exactly the same places. Other elements of rhythm in narrative are less physical and far more difficult to quantify, having to do not with an audible repetition, but with the pattern of the narrative itself. These elements are longer, larger, and very much more elusive.

Rhythm is repetition. Poetry can repeat anything—a stress-pattern, a phoneme, a rhyme, a word, a line, a stanza. Its formality gives it endless liberty to establish rhythmic structure.

What is repeatable in narrative prose? In oral narrative, which generally maintains many formal elements, rhythmic structure may be established by the repetition of certain key words, and by grouping events into similar, accumulative semi-repetitions: think of "The Three Bears" or the "Three Little Pigs." European story uses triads; Native American story is more likely to do things in fours. Each repetition both builds the foundation of the climatic event, and advances the story.

Story moves, and normally it moves forward. Silent reading doesn't need repetitive cues to keep the teller and the hearers oriented, and people can read much faster than

they speak. So people accustomed to silent reading generally expect narrative to move along pretty steadily, without
formalities and repetitions. Increasingly during the twentieth century readers have been encouraged to look at a
story as a road we're driving, well paved and graded and
without detours, on which we go as fast as we possibly can,
with no changes of pace and certainly no stops, till we get
to—well—to the end, and stop.

"There and Back Again": in Bilbo's title for *The Hobbit*,
Tolkien has already told us the larger shape of his narrative,
the direction of his road.

The rhythm that shapes and directs his narrative is noticeable, was noticeable to me, because it is very strong and
very simple, as simple as a rhythm can be: two beats.
Stress, release. Inbreath, outbreath. A heartbeat. A walking
gait. But on so vast a scale, so capable of endlessly complex
and subtle variation, that it carries the whole enormous
narrative straight through from beginning to end, from
There to Back Again, without faltering. The fact is, we *walk*
from the Shire to the Mountain of Doom with Frodo and
Sam. One, two, left, right, on foot, all the way. And back.

What are the elements that establish this long-distance
walking pace? Which elements recur, are repeated with
variations, to form the rhythms of prose? Those that I am
aware of are: Words and phrases. Images. Actions. Moods.
Themes.

Words and phrases, repeated, are easy to identify. But
Tolkien is not, after all, telling his story aloud; writing prose
for silent, and sophisticated, readers, he doesn't use key
words and stock phrases as storytellers do. Such repetitions

would be tedious and faux-naïve. I have not located any "refrains" in the trilogy.

As for imagery, actions, moods, and themes, I find myself unable to separate them usefully. In a profoundly conceived, craftily written novel such as The Lord of the Rings, all these elements work together indissolubly, simultaneously. When I tried to analyze them out, I just unraveled the tapestry and was left with a lot of threads, but no picture. So I settled for bunching them all together. I noted every repetition of any image, action, mood, or theme, without trying to identify it as anything other than a repetition.

I was working from my impression that a dark event in the story was likely to be followed by a brighter one (or vice versa); that when the characters had exerted terrible effort, they then got to have a rest; that each action brought a reaction, never predictable in nature, because Tolkien's imagination is inexhaustible, but more or less predictable in kind, like day following night, and winter after fall.

This "trochaic" alternation of stress and relief is of course a basic device of narrative, from folk tales to War and Peace; but Tolkien's reliance on it is striking. It is one of the things that makes his narrative technique unusual for the mid-twentieth century. Unrelieved psychological or emotional stress or tension, and a narrative pace racing without a break from start to climax, characterize much of the fiction of the time. To readers with such expectations, Tolkien's plodding stress/relief pattern seemed, and seems, simplistic, primitive. To others, it may seem a remarkably simple, subtle technique of keeping the reader going on a long and ceaselessly rewarding journey.

I wanted to see if I could locate the devices by which Tolkien establishes this master rhythm in the trilogy; but the idea of working with the whole immense saga was terrifying. Perhaps some day I or a braver reader can identify the larger patterns of repetition and alternation throughout the narrative. I narrowed my scope to one chapter, the eighth of Volume I, "Fog on the Barrow Downs": some fourteen pages, chosen almost arbitrarily. I did want there to be some traveling in the selection, journey being such a large component of the story. I went through the chapter noting every major image, event, and feeling-tone, in particular noting recurrences or strong similarity of words, phrases, scenes, actions, feelings, and images. Very soon, sooner than I expected, repetitions began to emerge, including a positive/negative binary pattern of alternation or reversal.

These are the chief recurrent elements I listed (page references are to the George Allen & Unwin edition of 1954):

- A vision or vista of a great expanse (three times: in the first paragraph; in the fifth paragraph; and on p. 157, when the vision is back into history)
- The image of a single figure silhouetted on the sky (four times: Goldberry, p. 147; the standing stone, p. 148; the barrow-wight, p. 151; Tom, pp. 153 and 154. Tom and Goldberry are bright figures in sunlight; the stone and the wraith are dark looming figures in mist)
- Mention of the compass directions—frequent, and often with a benign or malign connotation

- The question "Where are you?" three times
(p. 150, when Frodo loses his companions, calls,
and is not answered; p. 151, when the barrow-
wight answers him; and Merry, on p. 154, "Where
did you get to, Frodo?" answered by Frodo's "I
thought that I was lost," and Tom's "You've found
yourself again, out of the deep water.")
- Phrases describing the hill country through which
they ride and walk, the scent of turf, the quality of
the light, the ups and downs, and the hilltops on
which they pause: some benign, some malign
- Associated images of haze, fog, dimness, silence,
confusion, unconsciousness, paralysis (foreshad-
owed on p. 148 on the hill of the standing stone,
intensified on p. 149 as they go on, and climaxing
on p. 150 on the barrow), which reverse to images
of sunlight, clarity, resolution, thought, action
(pp. 151–153)

What I call reversal is a pulsation back and forth
between polarities of feeling, mood, image, emotion, action—examples of the stress/release pulse that I think is
fundamental to the structure of the book. I listed some of
these binaries or polarities, putting the negative before the
positive, though that is not by any means always the order
of occurrence. Each such reversal or pulsation occurs more
than once in the chapter, some three or four times.

darkness/daylight
resting/traveling on
vagueness/vividness of perception

confusion of thought/clarity
sense of menace/of ease
emprisonment or a trap/freedom
enclosure/openness
fear/courage
paralysis/action
panic/thoughtfulness
forgetting/remembering
solitude/companionship
horror/euphoria
cold/warmth

These reversals are not simple binary flips. The positive causes or grows from the negative state, and the negative from the positive. Each yang contains its yin, each yin contains its yang. (I don't use the Chinese terms lightly; I believe they fit with Tolkien's conception of how the world works.)

Directionality is extremely important all through the book. I believe there is no moment when we don't know, literally, where north is, and in which direction the protagonists are going. Two of the windrose points have a pretty clear and consistent emotional value: east has bad connotations, west is benign. North and south vary more, depending on where we are in time and space; in general I think north is a melancholy direction and south a dangerous one. In a passage early in the chapter, one of the three great "vistas" offers us the whole compass view, point by point: west, the Old Forest and the invisible, beloved Shire; south, the Brandywine River flowing "away out of the knowledge of the hobbits"; north, a "featureless and shad-

-owy distance"; and east, "a guess of blue and a remote white glimmer . . . the high and distant mountains"—where their dangerous road will lead them.

The points of the Native American and the airplane compass—up and down—are equally firmly established. Their connotations are complex. Up is usually a bit more fortunate than down, hilltops better than valleys; but the Barrow-downs—hills—are themselves an unlucky place to be. The hilltop where they sleep under the standing stone is a bad place, but there is a *hollow* on it, as if to contain the badness. Under the barrow is the worst place of all, but Frodo gets there by climbing *up* a hill. As they wind their way downward, and northward, at the end of the chapter, they are relieved to be leaving the uplands; but they are going back to the danger of the Road.

Similarly, the repeated image of a figure silhouetted against the sky—above seen from below—may be benevolent or menacing.

As the narrative intensifies and concentrates, the number of characters dwindles abruptly to one. Frodo, afoot, goes on ahead of the others, seeing what he thinks is the way out of the Barrow-downs. His experience is increasingly illusory—two standing stones like "the pillars of a headless door," which he has not seen before (and will not see when he looks for them later)—a quickly gathering dark mist; voices calling his name (from the eastward); a hill, which he must climb "up and up," having (ominously) lost all sense of direction. At the top, "It was wholly dark. 'Where are you?' he cried out miserably." This cry is unanswered.

When he sees the great barrow loom above him, he re-

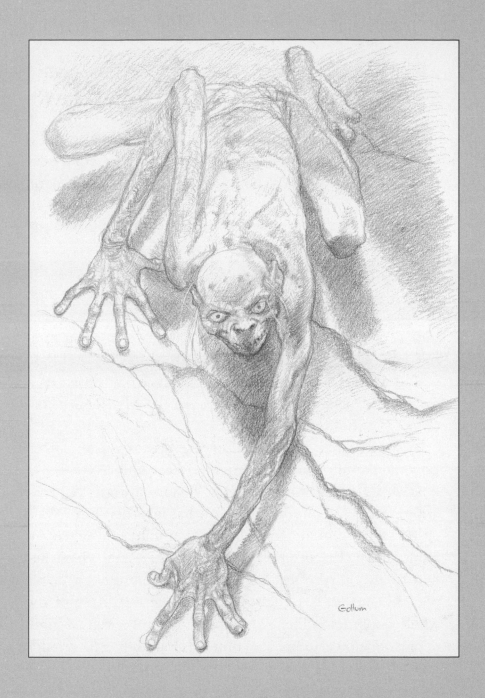

GOLLUM COMING DOWN THE CLIFF

The Two Towers

Book 4, Chapter I: "The Taming of Smeagol"

peats the question, "angry and afraid," " 'Where are you?' " And this time he is answered, by a deep, cold voice out of the ground.

The key action of the chapter, inside the barrow, involves Frodo alone in extreme distress, horror, cold, confusion, and paralysis of body and will—pure nightmare. The process of reversal—of escape—is not simple or direct. Frodo goes through several steps or stages in undoing the evil spell.

Lying paralyzed in a tomb on cold stone in darkness, he *remembers* the Shire, Bilbo, his life. Memory is the first key. He thinks he has come to a terrible end, but refuses to accept it. He lies "thinking and getting a hold on himself," and as he does so, light begins to shine.

But what it shows him is horrible: his friends lying as if dead, and "across their three necks lay one long naked sword."

A song begins—a kind of limping, sick reversal of Tom Bombadil's jolly caroling—and he sees, unforgettably, "a long arm groping, walking on its fingers towards Sam . . . and towards the hilt of the sword that lay upon him."

He stops thinking, loses his hold on himself, forgets. In panic terror, he considers putting on the Ring, which has lain so far, all through the chapter, unmentioned in his pocket. The Ring, of course, is the central image of the whole book. Its influence is utterly baneful. Even to think of putting it on is to imagine himself abandoning his friends and justifying his cowardice—"Gandalf would admit that there had been nothing else he could do."

His courage and his love for his friends are stung awake by this *imagination*: he escapes temptation by immediate, violent (re)action, and he seizes the sword and strikes at the crawling arm. A shriek, darkness, he falls forward over Merry's cold body.

With that touch, his memory, stolen from him by the fog-spell, returns fully: he remembers the house under the Hill—Tom's house. He remembers Tom, who is the Earth's memory. With that he recollects himself.

Now he can remember the spell that Tom gave him in case of need, and he speaks it, calling at first "in a small desperate voice," and then, with Tom's name, loud and clear.

And Tom answers: the immediate, right answer. The spell is broken. "Light streamed in, the plain light of day."

Emprisonment, fear, cold, and solitude reverse to freedom, joy, warmth, and companionship . . . with one final, fine touch of horror: "As Frodo left the barrow for the last time he thought he saw a severed hand wriggling still, like a wounded spider, in a heap of fallen earth." (Yang always has a spot of yin in it. And Tolkien seems to have had no warm spot for spiders.)

This episode is the climax of the chapter, the maximum of stress, Frodo's first real test. Everything before it led towards it with increasing tension. It is followed by a couple of pages of relief and release. That the hobbits feel hungry is an excellent sign. After well-being has been restored, Tom gives the hobbits weapons—knives forged, he tells them rather somberly, by the Men of Westernesse, foes of the Dark Lord in dark years long ago. Frodo and his companions, though they don't know it yet, are of course themselves the foes of that lord in this age of the world. Tom speaks—riddlingly, not by name—of Aragorn, who has not yet entered the story. Aragorn is a bridge-figure between the past and the present time; and as Tom speaks, the hobbits have a momentary, huge, strange vision of the depths of time, and heroic figures, "one with a star on his brow"—a foreshadowing of their saga, and of the whole immense history of Middle-earth. "Then the vision faded, and they were back in the sunlit world."

Now the story proceeds with decreased immediate plot-tension or suspense, but undecreased narrative pace and complexity. We are going back toward the rest of the book, as it were. Toward the end of the chapter, the larger plot, the greater suspense, the stress they are all under, begins again to loom in the characters' minds. The hobbits have fallen into a frying pan and managed to get out of it, as they have done before and will do again, but the fire in Mount Doom still burns.

They travel on. They walk, they ride. Step by step. Tom is with them, and the journey is uneventful, comfortable enough. As the sun is setting they reach the Road again at last, "running from South-west to North-east, and on their right it fell quickly down into a wide hollow." The portents are not too good. And Frodo mentions—not by name—the Black Riders, to avoid whom they left the Road in the first place. The chill of fear creeps back. Tom cannot reassure them: "Out east my knowledge fails." His dactyls, even, are subdued.

He rides off into the dusk, singing, and the hobbits go on, just the four of them, conversing a little. Frodo reminds them not to call him by his name. The shadow of menace is inescapable. The chapter that began with a hopeful daybreak vision of brightness ends in a tired evening gloom. These are the final sentences:

> Darkness came down quickly, as they plodded slowly downhill and up again, until at last they saw lights twinkling some distance ahead.
>
> Before them rose Bree-hill barring the way, a dark mass against misty stars; and under its western flank nestled a large village. Towards it they now hurried, desiring only to find a fire, and a door between them and the night.

These few lines of straightforward narrative description are full of rapid reversals: darkness/lights twinkling—downhill/up again—the rise of Bree-hill/the village under it (*west* of it)—a dark mass/misty stars—a fire/the night. They are like drumbeats. Reading the lines aloud I can't help thinking of a Beethoven finale, as in the Ninth Symphony: the absolute certainty and definition of crashing chord and silence, repeated, repeated again. Yet the tone is quiet, the language simple, and the emotions evoked are quiet, simple, common: a longing to end the day's journey, to be inside by the fire, out of the night.

After all, the whole trilogy ends on much the same note. From darkness into the firelight. "Well," Sam says, "I'm back."

There and back again. . . . In this single chapter, certain of the great themes of the book, such as the Ring, the Riders, the Kings of the West, the Dark Lord, are struck once only, or only obliquely. Yet this small part of the great journey is integrally part of the whole in event and imagery:

the barrow-wight, once a servant of the Dark Lord, appears even as Sauron himself will appear at the climax of the tale, looming, "a tall dark figure against the stars." And Frodo defeats him, through memory, imagination, and unexpected act.

The chapter itself is one "beat" in the immense rhythm of the book. Each of its events and scenes, however vivid, particular, and local, echoes or recollects or foreshadows other events and images, relating all the parts of the book by repeating or suggesting parts of the pattern of the whole.

I think it is a mistake to think of a story as simply moving forward. The rhythmic structure of narrative is both journeylike and architectural. Great novels offer us not only a series of events, but a *place,* a landscape of the imagination that we can inhabit and to which we can return. This may be particularly clear in the "secondary universe" of fantasy, where not only the action but the setting is avowedly invented by the author. Relying on the irreducible simplicity of the trochaic beat, stress/unstress, Tolkien constructs an inexhaustibly complex, stable rhythmic pattern in imagined space and time. The tremendous landscape of Middle-earth, the psychological and moral universe of The Lord of the Rings, is built up by repetition, semirepetition, suggestion, foreshadowing, recollection, echo, and reversal. Through it the story goes forward at its steady, human gait. There, and back again.

THE LONGEST SUNDAY

DIANE DUANE

I can see the morning sunlight now—the way it fell across the slightly faded, repetitively flowered yellow wallpaper of the dining room in the front of our house. It was 6:30 in the morning. I looked up, stunned by that sudden light intruding into darkness, having just come to the end of the second volume of The Lord of the Rings, and thought in utter horror:

There's another volume! And I don't have it!
AND IT'S SUNDAY!

Samwise lay on his face outside the shut gate. The war-arrow was making its way through Rohan. Gondor was about to be besieged. Dark shadows were abroad in the upper sky; Middle-earth was in deep trouble. And I was in nearly as evil a case, for the bookstore over in the next town, where I had bought the first two volumes of The Lord of the Rings, was now closed. This was the mid-1960s, in suburban New York, and in our neighborhood about the only things open on Sundays were churches.

Sam's despair had nothing on mine, I thought. And then I took the thought back, for Middle-earth, a world I had barely heard of a couple of days before, was now more important to me than my own.

I still don't know what made me buy the first two volumes and not the third. Did the bookstore guy (not an expert) really not *know* that there was another volume? Did *I* not know, or care? Even at this distant remove, I'd like to leave the bookstore guy some room for forgiveness. Sometimes, when I'm in a hurry, I'm not very observant. Did I genuinely miss any references to third volume? Did I pick this book up, dip in, realize that it was something special, and then just snatch up whatever was there and run out with it, heedless of minor matters such as extra volumes, but knowing I was onto something hot?

At that point, it didn't matter. I was in that peculiar torment known only to a dedicated reader who can't finish what she's reading. Being (luckily) a very fast reader, I had now become addicted to reading any given book in one sitting. The results of this could sometimes be comical if the subject matter was too radical or too exciting. I once got myself spanked, after one shattering afternoon spent reading *Starship Troopers* in its entirety, by going home from the library and immediately explaining to my father, with completely unconscious but rock-solid condescension, that all wars were caused by population pressure. I was nine at the time, and I still wonder about the unconsciousness (or sneaky boldness) of the librarian who shelved the book down in the children's library, right next to *Starman Jones*. More to the point, I tended to take my reading unusually seriously—possibly the reaction of someone who had been using it as a way to mitigate the effects of a fairly boring childhood. Then as now, reading as anodyne worked two ways: it both helped the situation and, occasionally, made it worse, by drawing other people's attention to the fact that a person "spends all the time with her nose in a book," as if there were some better place for one's nose to be (in someone else's business? Where it's not wanted?).

At the time, I was dimly aware that my parents regarded this leaning of mine toward escapism as slightly unnerving, possibly a sign of some instability. They had a slight case of something I've since seen more virulent cases of: a suspicion about the desirability of allowing kids to read fantasy—either because of an idea that the child might not be able to tell the difference between reality and fantasy, or because of the feeling that adults have some dire responsibility to keep the noses of the next generation firmly against the grindstone of merciless reality until they've lost beyond recall the ability to recognize that there are things worth escaping from, and places (real and unreal) worth escaping to.

I later, to my pleasure, discovered that Tolkien was under no illusions about this particular perception of "concerned adults": his feeling was that the people most concerned with or alarmed by the possibility of other people escaping, were jailers. But at the time, mostly I knew that I was imprisoned in a world I didn't particularly care for, and I looked forward to the day when I would be able to get out of the present set of circumstances. Meanwhile, I had to settle the issue of where I would go and what I would do with myself when it came time for college, and whatever would follow. And so I read voraciously, evaluating every possible option, finding out as best I could what the world was like, especially all parts of the world that did not look anything like a "bedroom community" in a suburb of New York City.

I explored the world remotely by more or less living, in my spare time, in that local public library. Other kids might chase me and call me a bookworm when I left, but while I was there, I was in sanctuary as certain as that of any church. And there was a whole lot more to read. Through books I explored deserts, oceans other than the Atlantic, faraway and exotic cities (even New York, where I was not yet allowed to go alone and which might as well have been as distant in time and space as Atlantis for all the good its presence only thirty miles to the west did me). Mountains, particularly, and especially the Alps, I looked at in pictures with the most intense longing, as somewhere I would eventually go, no matter what I did. They were almost a symbol of the real world, a world that was interesting and exciting and worth doing things in, even more effective for me as a symbol of the world than outer space—for the Moon landing of 1969 had moved me profoundly.

When I had started reading *The Fellowship of the Ring* I had no idea what was going to happen in it, or where it would take me. Mountains were there, and they delighted me . . . partly because they weren't just *there*: among them, things that suddenly concerned me deeply were happening to people and creatures who mattered. Shortly, the delight of faraway places was swept away in something much more important. All that Friday afternoon, after school, and Friday night until late, and all of Saturday and late into Saturday night, and then early on Sunday morning, I was completely and literally out of this world. And now, on this suddenly desolate Sunday morning, as I sat there in the sunny dining room, all alone—it was 6:30 in the morning, and no one was going to be up for a while yet—I found myself completely concerned with circumstances the likes of which I had never imagined, which made my troubles, and indeed just about every other trouble I knew anything about, seem petty and small by comparison. The idea that there were much, much more important things to worry about in the world than whether I was ever going to manage to grow through and out of a not terribly interesting or enjoyable childhood now descended on me full force. Suddenly I found myself confronting the issue of ultimate evil. It astounded me that I'd never particularly noticed it before. Now I realized that it had been sitting in front of me my whole life, like a rhinoceros in the middle of the living room, and I seemed to be required to take some kind of stand on the subject.

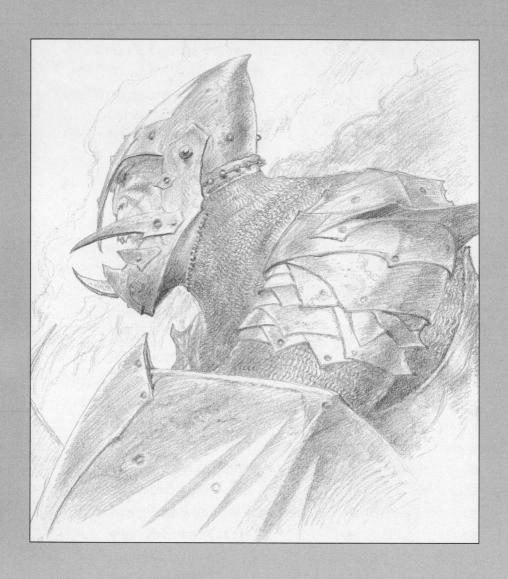

UGLUK, CHIEF OF THE ISENGARDERS

The Two Towers

Chapter III: "The Uruk-Hai"

I shied away then (and for a long time after) from considering who or what was doing the requiring at that point, or how my taking a stand could possibly make the slightest difference to the status of the world. That was a question I still haven't answered to my satisfaction. But on that Sunday, I didn't give the question more than few minutes' thought. I was completely overwhelmed at the thought of having to wait a whole day to find out what happened next. It was intolerable. My family watched me moping around the house, and wondered out loud, several times, what was the matter with me. Trying to explain was a mistake. My father just shrugged and said, "It's just a book; don't get so excited." And then rubbed in some salt by saying, "You should have taken your time and made sure there wasn't a third one before you left." Gee, thanks, Dad. See if I stand up for *you* the next time a giant spider stings you in the neck.

The rest of that day and that night (during which I got to sleep only late and with difficulty) dragged in a bad imitation of Einstein's joke-definition of relativity. But, finally, Monday morning manifested itself. I had to go to school first, which was even more of a nuisance than usual: the eight hours between going in there and getting out again looked wider than any desert and more challenging than any mountain. Caradhras the Cruel was on my mind—all that horrible ordeal the Company of the Ring had gone through, and for what?—and poor Sam lying there on his face, and Frodo, gone, alive, but maybe not to be so for long—who knew? I was shaking with nerves on this subject all day, for what had struck me as I read the first two volumes was a sort of merciless quality about Tolkien's writing—not so much a transparency of plot as an absolute subjection of it to the requirements, not of the author, but of the world he was writing about, or in. Middle-earth seemed to have its own agenda, to which maybe even Tolkien was, in a very special sense, in service, and it had occurred to me that happy endings might not be what that world was going to require of him, or me. I was terrified to get my hands on the third volume, and I couldn't wait.

Finally, time doing what it normally does in this universe, 3:30 rolled around, and I escaped from that place of torment at high speed, and ran to our little town's main street, and caught the bus to the next town, where the bookstore was. I threw myself in through its door and went straight to the rack where I had found the first two books, and found the third one, and seized it as if it was the heart out of my body, and just barely remembered to pay for it, for I was already reading it as I got to the door where the cash register was.

To this day I have no memory of how I got home. I was much more concerned with events on the plains of Rohan and at the tower of Cirith Ungo! And after finishing it that night, it took me a long time to get to sleep—I was suffering from a sort of jetlag of the soul. The world I lived in had been immeasurably broadened, but also somehow contracted by comparison with that other one—which was not "realer," for I wasn't deluded in the slightest on that count, but better. Yet having for the first time experienced a world so deeply imagined, I was also having to deal with an odd sense that it had been there for a long, long time . . . and also that, even after the book was closed, that world still existed somewhere else. That it would be there again when

I opened the book once more seemed almost an accident, as a room you've left will still be there (barring meteor strikes or other physical disasters) when you open its door again. At that point, at least, I was in no mood to leave the book closed for long. I started reading it again right away, and for about the next month probably would have been in serious contention for any award for the person who read the whole trilogy the most times in a week.

The Lord of the Rings was what started me on my present course of writing. I had always written stories to amuse myself, usually in the vein of whatever I was reading at the time—at that period the work was vacillating between what would now be considered fairly "hard" science fiction and the fairy-tale kind of story that E. Nesbit had done. But now I immediately began to write a series of wildly imitative and not very profound "epic fantasy" stories, and the Ring dominated my internal imaginative landscape for about the next twenty years. I still thought of the Alps, but now the great massif that included Celebdil, Fanuidhol, and Caradhras the Cruel was just as often on my mind; oceans still interested me, but the one across which one took ship from the Grey Havens had acquired more profound associations. The pain of that long, long Sunday faded quickly, and left me with something far better: a spare world to live in when this one occasionally became unendurable because of circumstance or boredom.

In the larger sense, life then proceeded to do what it usually does, and moved along, finally in some most unexpected directions. I went to college. I bombed out as a student physicist, but did well as a student nurse. I graduated with a preference for working in psychiatry. And as "work in the real world" went, that turned out to be satisfying, but also frustrating in some ways; and I had urges that nursing did nothing to satisfy. I kept writing, to the amusement, or sometimes bemusement, of those around me. Much to my surprise, I then mostly quit nursing, and went to work for a writer. And suddenly I got caught writing a book—a fantasy based in a vaguely medieval other-Earth, oddly enough. The book actually got bought by a publisher, and suddenly I was a writer, too. A joke around the household these days is that if I'd known how much the business of writing was going to cut into my reading time, maybe I wouldn't have gone on with it. But regardless of that, one book that still gets reread by me, at least once every year, is the *Ring*.

Eventually, I did make it to the mountains. I still remember well that first catch of the breath as I looked across the great vista of snowy peaks, a whole half-horizon of them, stretching away endlessly like waves of the sea: bigger than me, older than me, *realer* than me in some way; body and personality together suddenly seeming, in their presence, little, evanescent, and unimportant. It's a good experience, I think, one that I've had the chance to have fairly often in recent years. But the last time, I got something I wasn't expecting.

I was up on Mount Rigi, in the middle of Switzerland. It was spring. I was out for a walk one morning, to a place where that view is particularly good. There are no roads up there, just walking paths and meadows, and as I went by one meadow, I looked down into the grass and saw there something I hadn't been expecting: little, white six-petalled flowers, about an inch across. And a voice, Sam's voice, said in my head, "Do you remember the elanor, the sun-star, that we saw in the grass in Lórien?"

I got down to have a closer look. The little flowers turned out to be *Crocus alpinus,* the alpine crocus. But what the botanical references do not tell you is that *Crocus alpinus* throws a "sport" version in about one bulb of every twelve: a six-petalled version with little tips of pale gold at the end of the petals. They are unusual enough to make you search them out, once you start seeing them. They are (I think) elanor: for Tolkien holidayed in these mountains, and would certainly have seen them.

I straightened up from the little scattering of elanor and looked across the "back" of Rigi toward the higher mountains. If her devotees refer to Rigi (with some etymological reason) as "the queen of mountains," they do it also with a sense of rebellion, for in the background, from her peak, can be seen mountains of more regal, if not imperial, character: the Eiger, the Monch, and the Jungfrau. Tolkien hiked at the feet of those mountains, before he went to war. And when I stood up from seeing my first elanor, I looked across the great blue gulf of air and saw them there, as perhaps he did (for he would have ridden this cog railway, too): Celebdil, Fanuidhol, and Caradhras the Cruel; Silvertine, Cloudyhead, and the terrible Redhorn. For just a flicker of time, genuinely, physically, I was in Middle-earth.

Reality reasserted itself, but only with difficulty. I remember, a few breaths later, feeling maybe not so much a sense of kinship with Tolkien—that would have seemed impudent—but a strange sense of closure. And if I had been even slightly uncertain about the lasting power of his work, that uncertainty would now have vanished without a trace.

I started to wonder if the only way to judge the power of a writer's work is to look and see how thoroughly it "contaminates" the world in which its reader lives. When the words and images start insinuating themselves into unexpected parts of life, so that suddenly everything seems to refer back to that work, or remind you of things in it, then you know that a secondary creator of unusual skill has been at work *in* you. And when finding a concrete example of something "real," which the writer has drawn into his own world and made his own, suddenly makes the "real" world seem more magical than it actually is, that's wizardry of the most potent kind. The fact that The Lord of the Rings is indirectly responsible for (or at least involved in) nearly everything of value in my present life, fades to unimportance beside that best magic—the ability to make reality itself more real, to add something to it that wouldn't ever have been there otherwise, without one man's heartbreakingly inclusive imagination. Because of Tolkien, the universe will forever genuinely contain magic, even when all of it passes, and the covers of the book, for the last time, are shut.

TOLKIEN AFTER ALL THESE YEARS

DOUGLAS A. ANDERSON

Tolkien has long been an enigma to the critics, but not so to general readers. Sales figures are imprecise, but it was recently estimated that Tolkien's most popular work, The Lord of the Rings, has sold over fifty million copies worldwide in nearly thirty languages. And a number of polls in recent years have proclaimed The Lord of the Rings to be the book of the century. Personally, I find such polls and declarations to have little real meaning, but a simple truth does emerge that is undeniable, and that is that The Lord of the Rings is a novel much loved by a very large number of readers.

I first read *The Hobbit* and The Lord of the Rings in the summer of 1973, when I was thirteen years old. I was visiting my older sister, and pestering her in the usual ways in which younger brothers excel. I was also bored, and after looking over her bookcase and complaining that there was nothing to read, she stomped in from the kitchen, grabbed the Tolkien books from the bookshelf, and thrust them at me with a few staccato commands: "Here. Read these. You'll like them. Now leave me alone."

The books were those Ballantine paperback editions with the surreal Barbara Remington covers, showing a brightly colored landscape replete with emus, squiggly reptilian things, and trees with bulbous fruits. I looked at the books skeptically (as I still view those covers), but in my desperation I thought I'd try them. And I spent the next few days completely engrossed in those four books. Little did I then realize that I would spend the next thirty years studying those books, Tolkien's life, and his other writings.

My interests that have developed from reading Tolkien have shifted in many ways over these years. At first, I delighted in details of his world of Middle-earth, in the depth of the invented history and in the hints of partially told stories in the appendices. In high school, I wrote a play based on *The Hobbit,* which I performed with a number of my friends. And around that time I also began to read much more widely, both in the literature that inspired Tolkien (from *Beowulf,* the *Eddas* and the Icelandic Sagas, to the prose romances of William Morris), and in the modern writers, who were themselves in turn inspired by Tolkien.

At college I studied more seriously the medieval literatures in which Tolkien had specialized, and I even attended a summer program in Oxford, where Tolkien had lived and taught for much of his life. Through college and in the years that have followed, I have pursued whatever threads of scholarship that have interested me, many inspired by Tolkien, others not. This kind of freedom in my studies (possible only outside a prescribed curriculum) has led me down an unpredictable trail of study in the realms of mythology, fairy stories, and children's literature, followed by textual studies, bibliography, methods of printing, book production and publishing history, and many other areas beyond what is usually called literature and literary criticism.

I do not think my experience is atypical. Certainly it is not so among many of my Tolkienist friends and colleagues, for I believe that those of us who study Tolkien, and read his work very closely, find that his subtleties, his searching and penetrating intelligence, inspire our own interests to branch out in many unexpected directions. Of course, this observation is very much against the grain of the supposed truth that the critics of Tolkien have long proclaimed—that Tolkien fans read nothing but Tolkien, over and over.

To analyze the critical reception of Tolkien's works, one must first explain how much the bibliography of Tolkien's writings has greatly expanded since his death in 1973 at the age of eighty-one. During his lifetime, and for the moment excepting his academic work, Tolkien's primary literary publications amounted to only a small shelf of books: *The Hobbit* (1937); his short tale *Farmer Giles of Ham* (1949); the three volumes of The Lord of the Rings (1954–1955); the slim verse collection *The Adventures of Tom Bombadil* (1962); another slim volume, containing one story and an essay, entitled *Tree and Leaf* (1964); the short stand-alone fantasy story *Smith of Wootton Major* (1967); a song-cycle of Tolkien's poems set to music by Donald Swann, *The Road Goes Ever On* (1967); and an American paperback omnibus of some of these items called *The Tolkien Reader* (1965). Of all these titles, *The Hobbit* and The Lord of the Rings stand out as the major works, in size as well as in popularity.

Since Tolkien's death, an extraordinary amount of his previously unpublished writings have appeared, some finished, others unfinished. Very few writers have ever had their literary remains published to this extent, and presented with such exacting care as has been lavished upon these writings. Again temporarily excepting his academic work, since Tolkien's death we have been privileged to read some additional completed works for children, including *Mr. Bliss* (1982), and *Roverandom* (1998), both of which were illustrated by the author. Another volume, *The Father Christmas Letters* (1976; an expanded edition, retitled *Letters from Father Christmas*, appeared in 1999), reproduces in facsimile the stories and drawings Tolkien, in the guise of Father Christmas, made for his own children each year as they were growing up. In these letters Tolkien ingeniously developed an imaginary history for Father Christmas and the other denizens of the North Pole.

Despite the charms that each of the above books possesses, they remain lesser works when compared with Tolkien's greater achievement in his wide-ranging creation of Middle-earth; and it is in this latter area where Tolkien's posthumous publications are really so remarkable. Most of these volumes have been edited by Tolkien's third son, Christopher, who is almost uniquely qualified to oversee as literary executor the posthumous publication of his father's various writings, having the same literary background as his father and having a lifelong devotion to his father's writings. Christopher was a member of the original audience for whom *The Hobbit* was written, and he served as the first critic for his father as chapters of The Lord of the Rings were being written, some of which were sent serially to Christopher in South Africa where he was training to be a R.A.F. pilot during World War II. Christopher also followed his father academically, specializing in the same medieval languages and literatures. And like his father he taught these subjects at Oxford University.

The first major publication was *The Silmarillion* in 1977, an editorially constructed version of Tolkien's "Silmarillion" legends. (Here I follow the convention in Tolkien scholarship in referring to the published volume in italics, as *The Silmarillion,* while the "Silmarillion" in quotations marks refers to the evolving legends more generally.) This was followed by a collection of *Unfinished Tales* in 1980. From 1983 through 1996, Tolkien fans were given a new collection of Middle-earth writings nearly every year, the sum total being twelve large volumes of Christopher Tolkien's series on The History of Middle-earth. The resulting fourteen volumes—for one must include *Unfinished Tales* and *The Silmarillion* as part of the whole History—span nearly sixty years of Tolkien's creative work on his invented world. These volumes contain a multitude of fascinating things—a few completed, though most are not—varying in form from stories, essays, and annals to grammars, maps, illustrations, and poems (short ones, as well as long narrative poems in rhyming couplets or in alliterative verse). These works will be discussed below, but for now, suffice it to say that these fourteen posthumously published volumes contain roughly four times the amount of writing that is to be found in *The Hobbit* and The Lord of the Rings. Admittedly there is duplication and repetition, as well as some overlapping of contents (particularly in the volumes of the History, which cover the writing of The Lord of the Rings); nevertheless the simple amount of material on Middle-earth that Tolkien produced in his lifetime is staggering.

A few additional posthumous publications are worth noting here. *The Letters of J. R. R. Tolkien* (1981) is an enormously significant compilation in the field of Tolkien studies, for Tolkien's letter-writing style is in itself very engaging, and the letters (often written to fans, answering specific questions about his writings) reveal many otherwise unknown details of Tolkien's creation and his literary intentions. Taken together with Humphrey Carpenter's *J. R. R. Tolkien: A Biography* (1977), an authorized account for which Carpenter was given access to all of Tolkien's papers, the *Letters* and the biography are the two best starting points for an understanding of Tolkien as a literary writer. To highlight just one additional book, *J. R. R. Tolkien: Artist and Illustrator* (1995), by Wayne G.

LEGOLAS, ARAGORN AND GIMLI

The Two Towers

Book 3, Chapter II: "The Riders of Rohan"

Hammond and Christina Scull, shows another facet of Tolkien's skills, collecting a large number of his own drawings and paintings, many of which depict scenes and landscapes of Middle-earth, thereby giving another, visual, means to appreciate Tolkien's world.

To turn finally to the critical response, from the very beginning Tolkien's writings have evoked an initial reaction more emotional than intellectual. The reviews for *The Hobbit* at the time of its first publication are mostly pleasant, if occasionally a bit bewildered in trying to find a book to which to compare it. (In truth, none of the comparisons really work, for Tolkien was breaking new ground.) *Farmer Giles of Ham,* published twelve years after *The Hobbit,* didn't garner much attention at all. But a few years later, with the publication of the three volumes of The Lord of the Rings, the polarization of response to Tolkien began in earnest. Though The Lord of the Rings is in fact a single novel, it was split up into three volumes for marketing reasons, as the publisher hoped that three volumes, priced competitively, would get three sets of reviews, while a much higher-priced single volume would be reviewed only once, and probably sell fewer copies. The publishing strategy worked.

Some very big names, including W. H. Auden, Naomi Mitchison, and C. S. Lewis (who was also Tolkien's close friend), reviewed the books with high praise in high-profile periodicals, but others with equally big names did not like the books, and said so quite volubly. The single most notorious anti-Tolkien review is the one by Edmund Wilson entitled "Oo, Those Awful Orcs!" that appeared in *The Nation* in April 1956. In it, Wilson claims to have read the whole novel out loud to his seven-year-old daughter (yet he curiously misspells the name of a major character as "Gandalph") and calls The Lord of the Rings "essentially a children's book—a children's book that has somehow got out of hand, since, instead of directing it at the 'juvenile' market, the author has indulged himself in developing the fantasy for its own sake." Herein lies the basic charge that most other detractors of Tolkien have leveled against him in the years following. The problem, for Wilson, is that the book is fantasy, and he thereby attempts to marginalize it by saying it is for children. A study of Wilson's other critical writings shows that he had a marked dislike for almost any fantasy, although he did admit to liking the writings of James Branch Cabell, whose stories of Poictesme, a small imaginary kingdom of southern France, exhibit just the sort of risqué naughtiness and sexual innuendo that Wilson clearly expected to find in novels for "adults."

The controversy about The Lord of the Rings raged again in the mid-1960s, after the books were published for the first time in paperback in the United States, and they reached the bestseller's lists. But the basic argument against Tolkien remained mostly unchanged. The critic Harold Bloom has recently taken a slightly different tack in his dismissal of Tolkien, mistakenly confusing the widespread growth of Tolkien's popularity in the 1960s with the idea that Tolkien's works are thereafter to be considered as rooted in those times, culturally and historically. Bloom considers The Lord of the Rings to be what he calls (with capital letters) a "Period Piece"—presumably something that was once popular for some (to him) unfathomable reason, but was soon afterward forgotten. Bloom could not be more wrong.

The posthumous publication of *The Silmarillion* in 1977 was heralded by the media as an event, but aside from a few reviewers (notably Anthony Burgess and John Gardner), most critics compared *The Silmarillion* to The Lord of the Rings, and found it lacking in any of the charms of the latter book. *Unfinished Tales,* published in 1980, fared no better, and the subsequent twelve volumes of The History of Middle-earth have been studiously ignored by literary reviewers. In retrospect, one can see that, after the success of The Lord of the Rings, most serious criticism of Tolkien moved away from the mainstream newspapers and magazines and into specialist journals and books.

The critical antipathy to Tolkien is not merely a matter of genre but also of style and tone. The Lord of the Rings is really not, by more exacting critical definitions, a novel, but it is, as Tolkien himself called it, a "heroic romance." The Lord of the Rings is an example of a genre that had its origins thousands of years earlier, in Homer's *Iliad* and *Odyssey,* in *Beowulf,* and in the Arthurian tales—a genre that by the early twentieth century had been marginalized, particularly after the rise of modernism in the 1920s and 1930s. The genre of romance didn't die out by any means, but had limped along quietly for a few decades. Tolkien's work is firmly rooted in this romantic tradition, but it is also a development of that tradition along the lines of modern novelistic conventions.

Just at the time when the proponents of realism had begun to dominate the literary world, along came Tolkien and The Lord of the Rings, his refashioning of the old genre.

And as regards tone, Tolkien's writings are markedly different from the predominantly ironic trend in modern works. Tolkien was not incapable of irony, but he did not write in a largely ironic tone. Thus Tolkien's work represents much of what the modernists (and after them, the postmodernists) simply detest—and what is perhaps to them the worst offense of all, Tolkien's works have become popular.

To the book-buying public, the success of The Lord of the Rings in the mid-1960s inspired a revival of the older romance genre under the new name of fantasy literature. Tolkien's paperback publisher in America, Ballantine Books, responded to the increased demand for more things like Tolkien with a new series of Ballantine Adult Fantasy. The Ballantine series reprinted a large number of obscure books from earlier in the century, showing indeed that the genre of romance had by no means died out, but had moved along in the shadows of the more dominant literary forms. The series brought to a new audience the writings of such authors, now considered among the titans of the genre, as E. R. Eddison, Lord Dunsany, David Lindsay, and Mervyn Peake. And the market for new works of fantasy grew in leaps and bounds. The consideration of these post-Tolkienian fantasies I will leave for others, but I do note that many of the problems of these works have to do with the commercial success of fantasy, and of the genre thereby becoming an industry or commodity. As Ursula K. Le Guin has aptly written: "Commodified fantasy takes no risks: it invents nothing, but imitates and trivializes. It proceeds by depriving the old stories of their intellectual and ethical complexity, turning their action into violence, their actors to dolls, and their truth-telling to sentimental platitude."

The academic response to Tolkien has been nearly as problematic as the critical one, for in many instances the critics and the academics are the same people. As well, much of the modern literary education at universities has become so narrowly focused that one can without exaggeration say that readers are educated away from Tolkien by the conventional literary establishment.

Yet Tolkien has over the years made small inroads into the curriculums of some English departments. And his writings have been more widely appreciated in the specialized field of medieval studies, where a significant number of today's medieval scholars credit Tolkien with having been an inspiration in their choice of careers.

Academic criticism of Tolkien began in the sixties, and reached its highest point in the period before Tolkien's death with Paul Kocher's *Master of Middle-earth* (1972), a critical book that was also a popular success. Kocher's book has long been superceded, but it retains merit. In the years since, there have been quite a number of scholarly books on Tolkien. The best of these books are Tom Shippey's *The Road to Middle-earth* (1982), and Verlyn Flieger's *A Question of Time: J. R. R. Tolkien's Road to Faërie* (1997). *The Road to Middle-earth* is a comprehensive look at Tolkien's use of language and at how medieval languages and literatures influenced him, while *A Question of Time* explores comprehensively some smaller aspects of Tolkien, specifically his concerns with time and with dreams and how he used these elements in his fiction to deal with issues of the times in which he lived. But even these highly intellectual studies of Tolkien are for readers already sympathetic to him—in effect, they preach to the converted. Not so Tom Shippey's newest book, contentiously entitled *J. R. R. Tolkien: Author of the Century* (2000), which discusses Tolkien in relation to other modern writers such as George Orwell and James Joyce. Shippey presents a strong case for Tolkien being studied as a major modern writer, but whether the anti-Tolkien faction will even read this book remains a major question.

What is distressing is not the fact that these critics have dissenting views about Tolkien (and about fantasy), but that in the competition over the syllabuses at universities, and in the proposing of a literary canon, they seek to exclude anything that doesn't fall within their own narrow range of sympathies. And thereby they attempt to exclude Tolkien.

Leaving the critics aside, it is time to turn attention to just what understanding of Tolkien we gain from all of the posthumous publications, including his *Letters* and the History of Middle-earth series. First, it is worth pointing out a fact that is often overlooked, which is that Tolkien was not a writer by profession, and that he did not make his living by writing stories. He was a distinguished professor at Oxford University, where he held two chairs successively, first as the Rawlinson Bosworth Professor of Anglo-Saxon from 1925–1945, second as the Merton Professor of English Language and Literature from 1945 until his retirement in 1959.

Tolkien's contributions to his own scholarly field were not especially numerous during his lifetime, but they were of a high quality. Among them are *A Middle English Vo-*

cabulary (1922), designed for use with Kenneth Sisam's *Fourteenth Century Verse and Prose* (1921), an edition (co-edited with E. V. Gordon) of the Middle English poem *Sir Gawain and the Green Knight* (1925), and an edition of the *Ancrene Wisse* (1962), a thirteenth-century guide for women who lived as religious recluses in cells adjoining churches. Tolkien's lecture "Beowulf: The Monsters and the Critics," delivered to the British Academy in 1936, is a landmark in the study of Anglo-Saxon poems.

A number of his academic works have also come out posthumously, including his translations of three Middle English poems, *Sir Gawain and the Green Knight, Pearl,* and *Sir Orfeo* (1975), and a volume of scholarly essays, *The Monsters and the Critics and Other Essays* (1983). Some of Tolkien's lecture notes and working editions have also been published, including *The Old English Exodus* (1981), edited by Joan Turville-Petre, and *Finn and Hengest* (1982), edited by Alan Bliss.

Tolkien's posthumous writings on Middle-earth, it must be admitted, are not always easy reading. Within the invented world, Tolkien's writings begin with legends of the creation of the world, moving forward in time from there through three full ages of history. These writings tell of the wars with the first dark lord, Morgoth, which span the entire First Age; of the Atlantis-like story of Númenór, and its sinking near the end of the Second Age; and of the stories of the Third Age, including *The Hobbit* and The Lord of the Rings, which tell of the eventual downfall of Sauron, a follower of Morgoth who set himself up as a second dark lord. Some of Tolkien's Middle-earth writings transcend the age structure, as do some of his works on the languages, and the extraordinary short cosmological essay with diagrams, "Ambarakanta" ("The Shape of the World").

Tolkien's writings on Middle-earth range in date from around 1915 until his death in 1973; and in Christopher Tolkien's presentation, they are arranged mostly in a chronological order as to when they were written or worked on. With the publication of these writings we can now view as if from above the development of Tolkien's entire legendarium, which began, as Tolkien himself frequently recalled, as a vehicle for his invented languages. Tolkien felt that for his languages to live and evolve like real languages, they must have a people to speak them. He began with his Gnomish and Qenya (later, Quenya) languages, the speakers being elves. Tolkien envisioned a framework whereby an Anglo-Saxon mariner would sail overseas and be told stories by the elves, which he would later write up as "The Book of Lost Tales" after his return. Tolkien worked on these "Lost Tales" from around 1916–1920, after which time he concentrated on telling two of the major "Silmarillion" stories, those of Túrin and of Beren and Lúthien, in narrative verse. His "Lay of the Children of Húrin" reached more than 2,000 lines of alliterative verse, while "The Lay of Leithian" grew to more than 4,000 lines of octosyllabic couplets. Both are considerable expansions of their respective stories as told in "The Book of Lost Tales," and both remained unfinished.

Around 1926, Tolkien wrote out a prose "Sketch of the Mythology," which was for him the original "Silmarillion," later expanded and rewritten a number of times. By this time the essential core of stories related in the "Silmarillion" had been achieved, despite the fact that these stories would be rewritten in various forms over many years.

In the early 1930s, Tolkien wrote for his children the story *The Hobbit,* and in it, Tolkien freely used some characters (such as Elrond), places, and stories from his already existing mythology. He would later refer to this development as "the world into which Mr. Baggins strayed." For *The Hobbit* was intended to be a separate work, but as he wrote it, elements from the "Silmarillion" crept in. After *The Hobbit* was published and proved successful, Tolkien was asked for a sequel. The resulting novel, The Lord of the Rings, is as much a sequel to *The Hobbit* as it is a sequel to the whole "Silmarillion" legendarium.

Initially, Tolkien's invented mythology had been a closed thing, with a beginning, a middle, and an end, like the *Gylfaginning,* the first part of the thirteenth-century prose *Edda* of Snorri Sturluson, which sums up the Old Norse mythology, and which was an inspiration to Tolkien. Gradually, however, the end to Tolkien's mythology receded, and his invented history grew with the stories of later ages, including that of the Third Age, whose end is related in The Lord of the Rings.

Tolkien began work on The Lord of the Rings in 1937, and reached the end of the narrative twelve years later, in 1949. For a few years he worked diligently on the "Silmarillion," hoping to be able to publish it along with The Lord of the Rings as one large "Saga of the Three Jewels and the Rings of Power." In the end, only The Lord of the Rings came out at that time, and much of Tolkien's extensive writings intended for the appendices had to be omitted.

The volumes of the History of Middle-earth series, which cover the writing of The Lord of the Rings, are a special treat, for in them we learn a great deal about how Tolkien worked as a writer. Christopher Tolkien's account—in essence the history of the writing of a book—is unlike any other literary history, for in it we see the authorial process itself at work, and in great detail. Tolkien made many hasty notes to himself, and lengthy outlines, about the direction of the story, about why it could or couldn't go such and such a way. All these thoughts and arguments are written out. We literally see Tolkien thinking on paper, and we can share with Tolkien the wonder and bewilderment of new characters appearing as if from nowhere. What a privileged viewpoint this is.

After The Lord of the Rings was published, Tolkien turned a considerable amount of attention to parts of the internal philosophy of his invented world. He examined in great detail many aspects of the nature of the elves, their marriage customs and ceremonies, and their nature within the world, their spirits, and the idea of elvish reincarnation. He explored ideas on the nature of evil, and the origins of orcs. Tolkien also worked on some of the external aspects of Middle-earth, particularly on its cosmology, for he came to view that the setting of his invented world must be within the physical universe as understood by modern minds. Thereby he came to feel that he should discard his genuinely moving myth of the creation of the Sun and Moon as the last fruits of the Two Trees in Valinor. Christopher Tolkien, in sorting through the various versions of his father's writings, wisely retained this legend in the published *Silmarillion*.

Tolkien spent a great deal of time after the success of The Lord of the Rings in trying to recast his "Silmarillion" materials in a publishable form, and in trying to perfect a framework in which he could present these disparate legends and writings. He was, all through his lifetime, deeply concerned with the method of transmission of his tales—with who, within the invented world, wrote them originally, be it either of the elven sages, Rúmil or Pengolodh, and how these tales have survived into modern times, through copies and translations made by hobbits, and preserved among hobbit-lore, or by other means. Tolkien seems never to have satisfactorily resolved this for himself, and in the published version of *The Silmarillion*, all remarks placing the writings in this sort of historical context were removed.

As mentioned above, some of the volumes of the History of Middle-earth series are not necessarily easy reading. First of all, the writings cover an enormous span of time, and the Tolkien who wrote in the teens was not yet the talented prose stylist that he would become in the thirties and forties. As well, Tolkien developed certain prose styles for the differing methods in which he attempted to tell his tales. One Tolkien critic, David Bratman, has divided up Tolkien's prose styles into four main types, and these distinctions are useful in describing the varied materials in Tolkien's legendarium. The first is Tolkien's novelistic approach, as is found in *The Hobbit* and The Lord of the Rings. The three other prose styles Bratman has labeled as the Annalistic, the Appendical, and the Antique. The Annalistic style is that found in the various "Annals" and in the published *Silmarillion*—a distant, quick-moving narration of events. The Appendical style is much more essay-like, as is found in the appendices to The Lord of the Rings; it is also the predominant style of Tolkien's letters, and many of Tolkien's late philosophical writings. The Antique is the most archaic of Tolkien's styles, found in the "Ainulindalë" ("The Music of the Ainur," the creation myth at the beginning of *The Silmarillion*), and in Tolkien's earliest prose writings, *The Book of Lost Tales*.

Within each of these four styles of Tolkien's prose there are some remarkable writings. But in his narrative mode, which is perhaps the most engaging to the general reader, several of the most interesting examples are found in the volumes covering the writing of The Lord of the Rings, including the otherwise unpublished "Epilogue," which ties up a number of loose ends from the story. Also of considerable interest is "The New Shadow," the single, tantalizing chapter that Tolkien wrote for a sequel to The Lord of the Rings. (It appears in the last volume of the History.)

One thing the History of Middle-earth series makes abundantly clear, which readers only versed with The Lord of the Rings might not have thoroughly grasped, is that at the heart of Tolkien's great legendarium, of which The Lord of the Rings is but the small concluding part, are the legends of the "Silmarillion." Tolkien created—or subcreated, to use his own terminology—an entire *world,* and few aspects of it escaped his scrutiny. From the peoples and places, to the languages, nomenclatures, and writing systems, to the artwork, the textiles, and the calendars, etc.—all sorts of things beyond a simple narrative text. This multiplicity of expression and sheer attention to detail is one of the primary points of appeal for many readers of Tolkien; and in another sense this appeal often extends into a desire for more detail, and for some form of participation with the invented world on the part of the reader.

As embarrassing as the hobbit drama I wrote at age fourteen might be for me today, it shows this common impulse of many Tolkien readers. Writers are inspired to write. Artists want to illustrate and make paintings of scenes and characters. Musicians write music associated with stories. Linguists interpolate the gaps in the evolution of Tolkien's languages. And filmmakers want to make movies.

Readers want to involve themselves, and use whatever interests and talents they possess in order to participate in some way in Tolkien's world. These writings invite such a participation in a way that few other works of literature do. And therein lies the power of Tolkien's magnificent creation.

As Tolkien fans, we stand today at a crossroad. Before us looms Peter Jackson's three multimillion-dollar films of The Lord of the Rings, the first of which is due for release around Christmas 2001. Beside us stands a worldwide readership of the three-volume novel upon which the films are based. Behind each of us is our personal experience of reading Tolkien, our favorite characters and passages, the scenes and images Tolkien's words have conjured up in our minds, and our joy in sharing these enthusiasms with others.

The future is a question mark. Tolkien's novel has survived one previous attempt at filming, the 1978 Ralph Bakshi "rotoscoped" version, made by intermixing some live action in with what is predominately animation. Even that film was intended as part one of a series of films, but no theatrical follow-ups were ever made after the box office failure of the first part. Another firm, Rankin/Bass, did make an animated musical television production of *The Return of the King* (1980), as a follow-up to a similar version of *The Hobbit* (1977). Of the Bakshi movie itself, and of the truly execrable television programs, the less said about them, the better.

Now Hollywood has opened its considerable pocketbook for a new live-action version, with all three parts filmed before even the first part is released. The promise of the new films is tempered by experience, and by an entirely proper wariness and skepticism over what Hollywood might do to the novel. There is a modicum of solace: whatever the final judgment may be on Peter Jackson's films, the novel will always be there.

What is probably more alarming than any prospective film is the fact that Hollywood's engines of hype and commerce have been whirring along at full throttle for some years already, long before the release of the first film. The juggernaut of action figures, toys, puzzles, games, mugs, cards, stickers, figurines, and things such as Gollum Happy Meals will soon be upon us. These things are licensed not by the Tolkien estate, but by Tolkien Enterprises, a Hollywood firm completely unconnected with the Tolkien family, set up to exploit the movie, trademark, and merchandising rights to *The Hobbit* and The Lord of the Rings, which Tolkien himself sold off a few years before he died. And along with the movie-associated hype will come the inevitable rehashing of stale puns (e.g., "J. R. R. Tolkien is hobbit-forming") which we will be forced to endure from the ill-informed, smiling, vacuous faces of the media. In my view, all of this simply cheapens what is special about Tolkien—to the general public, at least, whose opinions of Tolkien are not yet shaped or prejudiced. For myself, I'm nearly prepared to go underground for the next few years. (Notice to the media: I mean that metaphorically, not literally—no hobbit-holes for me, please.)

From this vantage point I wonder how the future will view Tolkien's novel The Lord of the Rings versus Peter Jackson's films of it. Are we, as Tolkien fans in the year 2001, doomed to the same inescapable fate as that of the fans of L. Frank Baum in 1939, just before the release of the Judy Garland musical of Baum's children's novel *The Wonderful Wizard of Oz*? Today it seems impossible to view Baum's book in any other way than through the lens of the film, titled more simply *The Wizard of Oz*. Judy Garland is forever Dorothy Gale, while Margaret Hamilton has become a cultural icon for her superb performance as the Wicked Witch of the West. How will Peter Jackson's choice of actors and actresses affect future Tolkien reader's perceptions of the various characters? And what about his choice of New Zealand to be the visual backbone of Middle-earth? Or to put it more generally, will Peter Jackson's vision become the lens through which our society views Tolkien?

For good or ill, I hope not. I find I'm rather a purist for the written word, and in particular for the novel The Lord of the Rings. That is the form in which Tolkien envisioned and, in turn, created his masterpiece, and that is the form by which it should be remembered. This view, however, does not mean that I will scorn Peter Jackson's films. The translation of a novel to the screen is a process fraught with difficulties, and in the case of a really long work, like The Lord of the Rings, compression and alteration are inevitable. But I do look forward . . . cautiously . . . to the results of Peter Jackson's efforts.

HOW TOLKIEN MEANS

ORSON SCOTT CARD

When, as a child, J. R. R. Tolkien was inventing Middle-earth, modernism had not yet reared its head. And since Tolkien's academic career kept him immersed in languages no longer spoken, it is no surprise that his fictions showed no particular awareness of the modernist approach to literature.

Yet when Tolkien declared his distaste for allegory in all

its forms, he was also rejecting modernism's ways of interpreting the meaning of stories—and, ultimately, of insert-
ing meaning into stories. Certainly the modernists did not
embrace the one-to-one correspondence of object and ref-
erent that typified medieval allegory. But in the long run,
modernism has led to a method of interpreting the meaning
of stories that, like allegory, amounts to decoding stories
instead of experiencing them.

Tolkien's stories resist this method of reading, which is
why standard literary methods invariably lead to empty interpretations of Tolkien's work. What does the invisibility
ring "mean" in *The Hobbit,* and how is that meaning different from the "meaning" of the One Ring in The Lord of
the Rings? Jigger this question as you will: How do we in-
terpret the metaphor of the ring? To what was Tolkien al-
luding in the surrounding culture when he used a ring as
the embodiment of power? And the problem is still the
same: the rings have no "meaning" outside the story in
which Tolkien employed them.

The ring in *The Hobbit* gave Bilbo Baggins the power to
be invisible; it also provided him with a dangerous traveling
companion in the form of Gollum, who felt (quite correctly)
that he had been cheated in the game of riddles. The One
Ring in The Lord of the Rings was forged by Sauron to give
its wearer mastery over the rings of elves, dwarves, and
men; and those who wear the ring can easily be captured
by the evil inherent in its power—not to mention that
Smeagol/Gollum still tags along, as dangerous as ever. That
is the *meaning* of the ring in these two works. It is what it
does. Tolkien did not intend it to "mean" anything more,
because Tolkien did not write his fictions to be decoded,

but rather to be experienced and kept whole in the readers' memory.

Of course you can "decode" Tolkien's fiction according to whichever lit-crit lens you happen to be looking through. That's why these methods have been so popular in the universities for several generations now—you can always find *something* that you can declare to be a metaphor or symbol or analogy, and, like someone on a psychic hotline, spin out endless interpretations that cannot be contradicted by the text. The postmodern methods—feminism, multiculturalism, deconstructionism—differ in that they look for unconscious encoded messages, and then get angry at or contemptuous of the author for what he is found to have "revealed" about himself in his text. But they still treat the text as something to be decoded.

Writers who have been trained to think of writing fiction as the process of encoding meanings into a text produce stories in which such symbols are carefully inserted at key points and in ways that careful readers cannot miss. When you find their symbols, you are usually left in no doubt that this is a symbol, which has a clear meaning to the author— and often to the characters as well. Even when the meaning is left ambiguous or vague, you are clearly told by the way these symbols are inserted—usually by their irrelevance to the main line of the story—that this object is fraught with meaning, and attention must be paid. Certainly we recognize the bits they've inserted in order to stave off the contempt of the postmodernists—ah, here's the bit that keeps the feminists from killing this story; and here's the bit to make sure the multiculturalists recognize the author as acceptable. The story itself is often an afterthought. Certainly that's the way literature is generally taught in the universities—the value (or lack of value) of the great stories comes from the messages that can be decoded.

Why, then, are Tolkien's ring and Gandalf's staff and the hair on little hobbit-feet and the magical Ent-water that Pippin and Meriadoc drink *not* "fraught"? Why is it that when literadors skewer these objects and hold them up for display, announcing what they "mean," we who love these stories turn our heads away in some embarrassment, as if they had just used their soup spoon to eat their mashed potatoes?

Because Tolkien, like most storytellers in most societies throughout history, values stories *as stories,* not as essays in disguise. Tolkien does not want you to read his stories, decoding as you go. He wants you to immerse yourself in the tale, and care about what the characters do and why they do it. He wants you to feel frustrated when the Steward tries to burn his son alive, and relieved when his son's life is saved. He does not want you to start wondering if this is some sort of undoing of the Christ myth, or perhaps an allusion to the Akedah, in which the father offers his son as sacrifice only to have the sacrifice stopped at the last minute, with the father himself serving as "ram in the thicket." He does not want you to think of how this is really an analogy to the way the authority-loving patriarchy destroys its male children. He wants you to rush headlong through the story to find out what happens next. To find out what these events mean *to the characters,* what results will come from them, what causes will later be discovered. Aha, he was using the Palantir of Gondor! Aha, Faramir will be unable to step into the role of leader, leaving the road clear for Aragorn without forcing a conflict between these two good men.

The only meanings Tolkien cares about are the meanings *within* the story, not extraneous to it. These devices are present in the story for the story's sake. There is no Freudian imperative to put new names on them in order to understand them. Tolkien has given them their right names from the start; and when he does switch names, it is for practical, not literary, reasons—Aragorn is also Strider, Saruman is also Sharkey, and Smeagol is also Gollum—because their role in society changes in the process of the story, and the revelation of identity is meant to revise the meaning of the story *to its participants* as well as to the readers. Those revelations change the meaning of the story *within* the story, and not just in English class.

There are literadors who recognize this, but regard it as a reason to treat Tolkien's work as "subliterary." Because it does not lend itself to being operated on with the tools of the trade, Tolkien's oeuvre is not worthy of treatment as serious literature. And, apart from the value judgment inherent in this attitude, they are correct. If by "serious" literature, you mean literature whose meaning is to be found upon the surface of the story like an exoskeleton, to be anatomized without ever actually getting into the story itself, then Tolkien's work is certainly not "serious."

What Tolkien wrote is obviously not "serious," but "escapist."

Those who read "seriously" have no possibility of escape. They are never inside the world of the story (or at least cannot admit it in their "serious" discussion of it—God forbid they should be caught committing the misdemeanor of Naive Identification). They remain in their present reality, perpetually detached from the story, examining it from the outside, until—aha!—the sword flashes and the literador stands triumphant, with another clean kill. It is a contest from which only one participant can emerge alive.

"Escapist" literature, on the other hand, demands that readers leave their present reality, and dwell, for the duration of the story, within the world the writer creates. "Escaping" readers do not hold themselves aloof, reading in order to write of what they have found. Escapists identify with protagonists, care about what they care about, judge other characters by their standards, and hope for or dread the various outcomes that seem possible at any given moment in the tale. When the story is over, escapists are reluctant to return to the prison of reality—so reluctant that they will even read the appendices in order to remain just a little longer in a world where it matters that Frodo bore the ring too long ever to return to a normal life, that the elves are leaving Middle-earth, and that there is a king in Gondor.

So there we have it: "serious" literature is a complicated business, requiring experts to extract meanings, while "escapist" literature is so simple it needs no mediation.

Wait. That's not how it works at all. On the contrary, "serious" literature is so simple that it can be decoded, its meanings laid out in essay form, while "escapist" literature is so complex and deep that it cannot be mediated, but must be experienced; and no two readers experience it the same.

AT HELM'S GATE

The Two Towers

Chapter IV: "Helm's Deep"

That is the great secret of contemporary literature, that to write with "meaning" in mind simplifies a story. Consciously created symbols and metaphors silt it up until it is only a few inches deep, and you can find the fish as they flop around, and pick them up with your bare hands. But those stories written without an extraneous meaning run fast and deep, and those who dive in and are carried along by the current can never, as they say, step in the same river twice.

The Sirens chapter is always the Sirens chapter, every time you read it. But the Inn at Bree is never the same place for any two readers, or even for the same reader at different times.

Oh yes, right, I know: those who love *Ulysses* find new wonders in it every time they read. To which I say, cool. Read it again and again, you lucky Smart People; you really have it over the rest of us poor peasants who find it to be one long tedious joke, which isn't very funny because it has to be explained. Pay no attention to us as we close the door to your little brown study and get back to the party.

My point is that *Ulysses* can be taught. But The Lord of the Rings can only be read. When someone takes you through *Ulysses* and discusses it in serious literary terms, you constantly get the pleasures of a cryptic crossword puzzle: Ah, so *that's* why this chapter was so unintelligible! But when you discuss The Lord of the Rings, each explanation takes you, not farther into the text, but farther out of the story. Instead of "aha!" you keep thinking "is that all?"

Here's why: "escapist" reading is by nature wild, while "serious" reading is by nature domesticated.

"Serious" reading is designed to bring readers to a

common experience *outside* the story, by writing papers that attempt to persuade others that *this* is the (or a) "meaning" of this or that item in the tale (or attribute of the text).

But "escapist" reading brings readers together only when they are *inside* the story; and the more closely they compare notes, the clearer it becomes that they have not had the same experience, not in detail.

This is not simply because readers inevitably come up with different visualizations of the characters and milieux—for the same difference between "serious" and "escapist" can be found in the ways people make and watch movies, which forbid you to engage your visual imagination.

Rather, "escapist" readings vary so widely because the story is not the text. Rather the text is the tool that the readers use to create the story in the only place where it ever truly exists—their individual memories. Because the writer has provided the same tool to all readers, the stories in their memories will resemble each other, sometimes very closely. Can we conceive of any reading of The Lord of the Rings that does not have the Gollum biting off Frodo's finger, and falling, finger, ring, and all, into the fires of the Cracks of Doom? But haven't we all had the experience of discussing the story with someone else and having him or her refer to some moment, some event, that we had forgotten, or never noticed, or—and this happens surprisingly often—that is absolutely contradicted by our own clear memory?

Readers, in fact, make a jumbled mess of their reading. Like eyewitnesses who only remember what they noticed, and only notice what seems important enough to command their attention at the time, readers edit unconsciously as they go, linking moments in this present story to moments in other stories that were inadvertently called to mind. (How many times have I heard readers praise or complain about a particular scene or phrase or event that simply does not occur in the book in which they say they remember it?) What reader, upon rereading a particular story, especially after an interval of several years, is not surprised to discover that *this* scene is in the same story as *that* scene?

When readers are not "serious," but rather are deeply, personally, and emotionally involved in a story, the story is transformed to at least some degree by their preexisting view of how the world works. They do not realize it at the time or, usually, ever. They *think* the story they love so much is Tolkien's story. But in fact it is a collaboration between the-Reader-at-This-Moment and Tolkien-at-the-Time-He-Wrote. Tolkien is the author: when there are disputes about what happened in the story, it is to Tolkien's text that disputing readers must return, with no extraneous commentator having even the slightest authority. But except for those rare moments of controversy or of the cognitive dissonance of rereading a familiar tale that turns out to be unaccountably strange, readers remain unaware of how they have transformed the tale.

Similarly, readers are rarely aware of how the tale transforms them. For that is the power of "escapist" (but not "serious," or seriously read) fiction: The events of the story, their causes, their results, their meanings-within-the-tale, enter into the readers' memory in a way that is ultimately only somewhat distinguished from "real" memories. In part, this is because "real" memories are in fact "storyized" whenever they are recalled or recounted, so that "real" memories become more certain even as they become less correspondent with the actual experience. But "escapist" readings gain most of their power to transform the readers' worldview from the very authority of the author.

While we live in Tolkien's world, it is with almost unbearable pain that we watch Gandalf fall to his death, locked in the embrace of the Balrog, or see the damage Sharkey and his gang have done to the once-lovely Shire. We have no doubt that Shelob must be stopped, not because she is part of Sauron's evil plot, but simply because she is in the way. We are allowed some pity for her, but Frodo *must* be freed. This is a morally complex issue, in fact. The more we examine it, the more our sympathy for Shelob increases. She isn't trying to rule the world, she's merely trying to eat. Isn't she in the category of the shoplifter who steals food because he's starving? Well, not quite—after all, her idea of a snack is Frodo, not a bag of Oreos. But to her, what is Frodo but lunch on the hoof? He is not of *her* species. If he gets stuck in her web, he's meat. What has she done that makes her worthy of death? And yet whatever pity we feel on first or second or third reading, the fact remains that we want her to fail; and because she is so relentless, the only way she can fail is to suffer incapacitating injury, and so we are relieved when she is hurt and retreats to her lair to suffer the agonies our heroes have inflicted on her.

This is a complicated process, and it is quite possible that Tolkien is creating or reinforcing an immoral morality. That is, if you subscribe to the worldview of the People for the Ethical Treatment of Animals (PETA), obviously, Shelob is an innocent victim, and The Lord of the Rings supports an evil anthropocentric view of the animal kingdom, in which humans (or ur-humans) have the right to intrude wherever they want and kill or hurt whatever animals happen to get in the way.

Yet there is no room within the experience of the story to argue with Tolkien. The Lord of the Rings is not an essay, whose tenets are to be consciously considered. It is a story, plain and simple; and if during the Shelob passages your deep morality is offended, the effect is not an argument, but rather a withdrawal from the world of the tale. You close the book—perhaps you throw it against the wall. Or perhaps you grit your teeth and return, because the rest of the story is so good that you'll just have to ignore the mistreatment of Shelob and move on.

That's what happens when a story is so foreign to our own worldview that we cannot accept it. The Escape is over. We are forced to return from the story because we cannot bear to live in the author's world any longer.

Often, we cannot name our reasons. It is nothing so plain as a PETA member's reaction to the Shelob story. Rather, we find our attention wandering when we try to escape in a story whose world is unbearable to us. Or we find ourselves losing our willingness to suspend our disbelief. Or we simply don't understand what's happening—we can't process the story, because the characters' actions don't make sense to us.

That's why stories can never be wholly transformative. The author makes things happen in a tale for reasons that are only sometimes consciously understood. But having created the story, having offered it to the public, the author may find that many people read it with enthusiasm, while a few find it tedious, unbelievable, incomprehensible, or even evil. The same book! So variously, even perniciously misread! But it is the simple result of the fact that no two individuals actually live in the same world. Oh, we think we do—we have conversations and share food and bicker and so on—but nothing ever means exactly the same thing to any two participants in an event. (Note that I'm referring to meaning-within-the-tale, though in this case the tale happens to be reality.) And even when we explain our view and achieve agreement, we have to admit that even our agreement has a different meaning to each and every person who agrees to it. We may agree that we agree, but in fact we do not fully agree.

All stories have to offer some common ground to at least some readers—some aspect of the worldview of the tale that feels true and right. Without that, the readers cannot escape into the tale for long. Indeed, my guess (though it cannot be measured) is that the vast majority of causal and moral assertions in the tale must already be shared by the storyteller and the culture that produced the readers who embrace it; it is within this flood of agreement that the author's unique (and therefore strange-to-the-readers) views are able to slip through unnoticed, subtly but often significantly changing the way the readers see the real world that they return to when the Escape has ended.

Oddly, it is in the reading of fiction that we come closest to achieving communication—true harmony of worldview. When you and I both read The Lord of the Rings (or any other story), we have the chance to share memories that were shaped by a single consciousness—in this case, Tolkien's. To the degree that we both take joy in his world and believe in it, to the degree that our worldview is transformed by Tolkien's, then to that degree we approach the possibility of understanding, the possibility of being, however momentarily, of one mind. We never actually achieve it, but the mere approach, like the approach to lightspeed, has wild and powerful effects. Where "serious" readings result in scholarly papers and learned lectures, "escapist" readings plunge us into experiences that cannot be codified, even though we understand that, having read this story, nothing will ever be the same for us.

Now, I must be fair about this: "serious" readers guiltily admit, when pressed, that along with their "serious" reading, "escapist" experiences sometimes slip in by accident—and they enjoy them, too. Perhaps even more than they relish the pleasures of successful decipherment. Is what the lovers of *Ulysses* love that which must be decoded, or is it that which does not need decoding, but which must instead be ("escapistly") experienced?

Fiction is valued in every human society precisely because it makes us who read it temporarily, approximately, One. We have memories in common—memories more complex and powerful than any but a few shared rituals can provide. And when a society embraces stories that create or reinforce worldviews that lead people to behave in valuable ways—nobly giving their lives for their country, for instance, or responsibly taking care of their children's needs no matter how inconvenient or difficult that may be—then that society is more likely to survive than one whose stories create worldviews that celebrate a refusal to sacrifice for the good of others. And certainly it is worthwhile to examine just what the worldview is that the writer has (probably unconsciously, perhaps inevitably so) offered to the readers who embrace the tale.

But we must remember that such an examination does not decode a story, but rather concentrates only on the meanings-within-the-tale. We do not look for what Shelob "symbolizes." We look for what it means within the story's *own* terms that Shelob tries to kill Frodo and, ultimately, fails; what it means *in the story* that Sam wears the ring repeatedly in order to search for Frodo and free him; what it means when Frodo snatches the ring back from Sam. Our judgment is not aesthetic, ultimately, but rather moral. (It can be argued, of course, that aesthetic judgments are all, ultimately, moral judgments, for reasons that should suggest themselves in what I have already said here.)

And we must also remember that honest, careful readers can still disagree about the same, beloved story. For instance, the denouement of The Lord of the Rings is extraordinarily complex. The ring has been destroyed, Aragorn enthroned, the Shire scoured. But Frodo is not happy in the Shire. He wore the ring too long. It scarred him. For him, joy can only come by leaving what used to be his home and sailing into the West with the elves, to a land of heroes and myths. His is a bittersweet parting, very much like death, very much like going to heaven. No, I am not retreating into decipherment. But Tolkien was a convert to Catholicism, and the deep story of Catholicism was a part of his worldview. It is bound to show up in his stories, not in an allegorical, conscious, encoded way, but rather as the-way-things-work. When you have borne such a deep, soul-scarring burden, it cannot be healed in Middle-earth. Frodo has stared into hell as no other living soul has done; he can only be healed and become whole in the West. This is not allegory, it is honesty—it is Tolkien telling the truth, not by plan, but because this is what felt right and true to him as he was making the thousand unconscious decisions that a writer makes on every page of every story.

We are meant to shed tears (or to wish to shed tears), as believers would at the deathbed or funeral of a good soul of whose eternal happiness we have no doubt.

And if that had been the only ending of The Lord of the Rings, I don't know if I would love this story the way I do. Because of course there is another ending, one that Tolkien no doubt thought of as "second prize": Sam's return to the Shire, and *his* happiness there.

Most readers of The Lord of the Rings I have talked to, you see, regard Frodo as the great hero of the book, and certainly that is what the text would lead any rational person to believe. But I, and a certain subset of readers of The Lord of the Rings, don't see it that way. When I read the story, with the great climactic scene at the Cracks of Doom, I saw Frodo as a failure. When he reached the moment of choice, *he could not do it.* He did not walk on his own legs to that place, he was carried there; and when it was time to let go of the ring and see it fall to its destruction, he instead declared himself the ringmaster and put the damned thing on. The ring won. It was stronger than Frodo. He failed.

Most people accept this as Tolkien clearly intended—after all, he has told us more than once that, without naming God, *someone* was planning these events, and had a role for Gollum to play, and that role was to bite off the finger and its ring from the hand of the failed ringbearer, and then die along with the ring he loved so much. In other words, no man, not even Frodo, had the power to do what had to be done, and only because it was *meant* to happen did the ring end up being destroyed.

Here's my eccentric reading (which is also justified in the text, but with different emphasis): There was one ring-bearer who voluntarily, willingly surrendered the ring after having worn it repeatedly: Samwise Gamgee. It was Sam, not Frodo, who actually carried the ring those last miles to the Cracks of Doom, by carrying Frodo who carried the ring. There is no analogue to Sam in the Christ story (which is one reason why allegorical readings of The Lord of the Rings fall apart). Nobody picked Christ up and carried him to his sacrifice. Yet something in Tolkien knew that the ring was too terrible for Frodo to carry it himself, right to the end. Maybe it was, in Tolkien's mind, something as trivial as the necessity of the plot—having written that Frodo was carried off from Shelob's lair by the Orcs, the only way he could think of for Frodo to get free was for Sam to put on the ring. Whatever Tolkien's conscious reasoning was, however, the fact remains that Sam was also a ringbearer. But because he was of a humbler social class, he never once conceived himself as being truly worthy to bear it. Oh, the ring worked its magic on him, and he had his moments of imagining what such power in his hands might accomplish. But he knew that even these wild dreams were humble and silly (in the ancient meaning of the word), and his humility made him laugh at his own ambitions.

Samwise Gamgee was, in fact, the quintessential servant, and no doubt there was something in Tolkien that resonated with the idea that "whoever would be greatest

among you, let him be the servant of all." By such reck-
oning, it is Sam, not Frodo, who was the greatest of the
heroes—and all the greater, I felt at least, because it never
crosses Sam's mind or anyone else's that this might be the
case. Indeed, Sam is so purely focused on the greatness of
his master that it is almost impossible actually to consider
him for himself; he exists only in relation to Frodo. It is not
until Frodo sails to the West and Sam returns home that at
last he is freely and fully himself. Now at last the servant is
master in his own home, able to take joy in the company
of his wife and children, to labor happily in his garden, and
watch and take part in the blossoming of his beloved land
and his beloved neighbors.

In my reading of the story—and remember, this was my
original, natural reading, not analyzed, simply the way I
took the story—Sam was the great hero; and The Lord of
the Rings had a perfect ending because he was, finally, the
only ringbearer who had no regrets. He had borne the ring
but had done nothing wrong with it; and despite temptation, he had surrendered it more freely than anyone who
had ever worn it. So it was fitting that he received, not the
contemplative life of Frodo's apotheosis, but rather the idea
of heaven that I had grown up with in my definitely non-
Catholic religion: to live in a garden made by his own
hands, surrounded by his family, and able to watch and
help his family and his garden improve and increase.

Certainly everything I saw in the story is there. But over
the years I have found that most people receive the story
as Frodo's, and his passage into the West as the ending, with
Sam's return to the Shire as simply a way of putting period
to the tale. Still, a significant number of readers do agree

with me in my admittedly eccentric reading, in which Frodo's passage west is sad, a melancholy end to an injured soul, while the true ending of the story is Sam's return home as a man at last unsubservient (and yet still serving), who deserves his true happiness because he is the only one who obeyed and acted nobly in all cases, even when his first desire was otherwise.

This is not some coded meaning, it is how I experienced the meaning of these events within the world of the tale. These events did not "stand for" anything in the real world. But my own worldview caused me to receive the story with different emphasis, different moral weight, different values from the way many others received it. It is not even terribly interesting what Tolkien "meant" as he wrote it; to the degree that his choices were unconscious, they can be trusted to reflect what he truly believed; and to the degree that his choices were conscious, they can be trusted only to show us what he believed that he believed.

In this case, as with most elements of The Lord of the Rings, I assume Tolkien to have been writing "escapistly," without encryption, deciding what happened and why, solely on the basis of what felt important and true to him at the time he was writing or revising. I may well be projecting my own process of storytelling onto Tolkien because, inevitably, I always view the world through my own lens, having no other, no matter how I try to polish it and focus it clearly. But he said there was no allegory here, and I take him at his word, with the broadest reading of the term allegory, to include all methods of encryption and decipherment of extraneous "meaning."

The Lord of the Rings, like all of Tolkien's fiction and,

I believe, all truly great tales, is a wild tale, untamable. It is the mark of the depth of this great river that sweeps us along when we step into it that there can be variant readings, which are nevertheless consonant with the text. It is as ragged as a river, with sandbars here and there that fetch us up and leave us dry for a moment or two (I've never cared about the barrow-wights; and others have their sections or characters that bore or irritate them). But the river flows on, and when we leap back in we are caught up again; and if, in its broad delta, some of us end up in a different place when the story's over, well, that's what happens in such wild streams. In fact, that's what we hope for, that this author's world is so real that when we immerse ourselves in it, we can never be sure, from one reading to the next, where it will take us, or what we will see along the way.

We have run this river, you and I—more than once, in my case, and quite probably in yours. I keep returning to it precisely because it has never been tamed, and cannot be tamed. It is wild every time, and so the "meanings" of the story, while boundaried by the words on the page and the mind that envisioned the tale, are nevertheless many, each one a current that can tug me here this time, there the next, to see different meanings every time.

Forget the river metaphor. No analogizing now. There is a man's whole soul in the pages of this tale, a man's whole life, each stage of it, represented in the elements of its creation. The great storytellers are the ones whose characters become as real in our memories as our friends and family. As ourselves. I have lived in Middle-earth, and so have you;

and it matters to us, or you would not be reading this book, and I would not be writing this essay. All these years since Tolkien died, and yet he still reveals the world, the wide and wild world, to us.

THE TALE GOES EVER ON

CHARLES DE LINT

My first encounter with Tolkien was through my older sister, Kamé, when I was around twelve or thirteen. I'd temporarily put aside the fairy tales and books on myth and folk tales that I'd been reading (not to mention Edgar Rice Burroughs's Tarzan and John Carter books borrowed from my father's bookshelf) and had been seduced, hook, line and sinker, by mysteries and spy thrillers. Instead of Donkeyskins and cats in boots and Taliesins, my head was filled with the exploits of the Saint and Modesty Blaise, Shell Scott and Mike Hammer, Nick Carter and James Bond.

What can I say? I was young, I was impressionable.

The day in question was probably on a weekend. A Saturday or Sunday. I came into my sister's bedroom (without knocking, I'm sure) and was hanging around being a pest when I noticed this book lying on her bed. *The Hobbit*. I asked her what it was about, and she proceeded, with great enthusiasm, to tell me about Bilbo Baggins and Gandalf, about dwarves and elves and Rivendell and all.

I'd like to say that I was immediately won over and put aside the hardboiled detectives and spies to immerse myself in Middle-earth, but it wouldn't be true. Instead, I laughed and made fun of her for reading kids' books (being so mature myself, of course).

And I should have known better. I mean, not only was Kamé first on the mark with Tolkien, she was also the first person I knew to have ever heard of the Beatles and to have gone so far as to get a couple of their 45s long before anybody else was even remotely aware of them. I mention this, because those 45s mesmerized me as much as Tolkien's stories did when I finally did read them. We used to listen to the Beatles over and over again, and when the band finally showed up on Ed Sullivan (hard to believe now, but back then that was the *only* show on TV where you could see anything like that), we were in heaven.

But I digress.

On the day she had borrowed *The Hobbit* from the library, and was almost finished reading it, Tolkien just seemed about the goofiest thing anybody could want to read.

I remember that clearly. I don't remember exactly when it was that I went on to read *The Hobbit* and The Lord of the Rings after that, but it had to be a couple of years later—still in the mid-sixties.

I was already familiar with some of Tolkien's source material, as I've mentioned above, but this massive story of his, with all the original touches and sheer veracity he brought to his work, was the point where I fell utterly head-over-heels in love with the idea of magic and wonder, and the effect it could have on an ordinary person (the hobbits, for all their furry feet and other charms, still stood in for everyman when compared to everyone and everything else in those books).

To say that it changed my life would be putting it mildly. It reawoke the child in me—not the innocent, but rather the boy capable of putting aside cynicism and able, once again, to regain his sense of wonder.

I can, and will in a moment, talk about the enduring appeal and value of those two books (I don't care that publishers created a whole misconception about fantasy and trilogies; in my mind, I follow Tolkien's lead and consider The Lord of the Rings a single book), but I'd like to explore for a moment what it was like to come across these books at the time I did, and why I reread them so often.

For one thing, there was the Story of it all. My previous experience with such material had only been in short formats—fairy tales, folk anecdotes, mythologies—that weren't entirely satisfying, though I doubt I could have explained it at the time. What I did know was that here was a huge story, a tapestry within which one could get lost for days. The characters were believable, not only because they were so well-drawn, but because they had reasonable motives for doing what they did. One of the least satisfying aspects of those earlier stories that Tolkien had used as source material (and which I'd also read) was how so much of it was arbitrary. The characters were too often simply archetypes, with no effort made to expand their personalities, their strengths and failings existing solely for the purposes of the story, rather than growing out of their own experience and history.

(An ironic aside here: Nowadays, many of those fresh and vital characters that Tolkien created, or refurbished from old folkloric and mythic material, have become the archetypes for fantasy fiction. The circle turns. . . .)

Because of my own inexperience (I'd yet to hear of Dunsany, Morris, Cabell, et al.), I'd never come across anything like this before. I know that sounds odd, writing this at the tail end of the year 2000, when the shelves of any library or bookstore are sagging with enormous, and too-often, bloated fantasies of a similar ilk. But the classics were still hidden to me, and the subsequent tsunami of Tolkienesque wannabes was still but a gleam in Ian Ballantine's eye.

Though to be fair, I owe Ballantine Books almost as much a debt of gratitude as I do Tolkien. If Tolkien showed me that fantastical, magical worlds were for all ages, the Ballantine Adult Fantasy line, under the editorship of Lin Carter, and with the Sign of the Unicorn in the top right-hand corner of each volume, showed me that there was far from one way to tell such stories.

Looking back, I think the most interesting thing about

THE DARK TOWER

The Return of the King

Chapter III: "Mount Doom"

these books was just that: how very different they were from one another. There was no mistaking Clark Ashton Smith's dark visions for the pastoral worlds of William Morris. Nor William Hope Hodgeson's Night Land for Hope Mirrelees' Faerie, even if they shared a given name.

This is probably the single strongest reason I have so little patience for much of the fantasy being published today. Coming upon those classics in my formative years spoiled me forever. Why would one want to read incessant variations on the same tired story—which, I'm sorry, but don't try to tell me that most fantasy novels of the past twenty years aren't pretty much an endless factory line of more-of-the-same—when an author could, and should, have his or her own individual worlds and stories to share with us.

But I've jumped ahead of myself.

At the time I first began to read Tolkien, June 1969 (when the Ballantine Adult Fantasy line began to bring the classics to the attention of hungry readers such as myself) was still years away. And while I already had experienced, or was soon to experience, Lloyd Alexander's Prydain series (1964 through 1968), Susan Cooper's The Dark Is Rising series (1965 through 1977; oddly enough, also a set of five books), Alan Garner's wonderful fantasies (such as *The Weirdstone of Brisingaman*, 1960) and others of their like, they were still aimed at a young adult/children's market—for all that older readers could, and still do, appreciate them.

I remember those books with fondness, and still go back to reread them from time to time, but they pushed different buttons for me. None of them had the scope, nor the truthfulness, of *The Hobbit*, and especially The Lord of the Rings. There were detailed maps of Middle-earth. Whole languages and histories. One could marvel in the rumor that Tolkien had created these stories simply as a setting for his true interest: creating his elvish languages. Subsequent books such as *The Silmarillion* and the many others to follow, each a little less readable than the one before for most readers, myself included, only seemed to bear this out.

We didn't so much feel that Tolkien was making up Middle-earth, as allowing us a glimpse into some alternate reality; and let's face it, at that time, alternate realities held a great deal of attraction for many of us growing up in what felt to be far too stifling a society. There were rules and regulations in Middle-earth, true, and much of what the books were about was a passing of innocence and Faerie, from this world into the next. But that didn't invalidate the feeling that there once had been magic in the world, and perhaps, if we looked hard enough, and worked hard enough, it could be regained.

Magic wasn't simply elves and wizards and spells. Magic also seemed to promise a deeper and more resonant connection with the world and all of us inhabiting it. It's not so surprising that the peace, love and flowers generation should have taken these books so much to heart. Tolkien was writing about the industrialization of his beloved England, but throughout the world we could find similar analogies. Mordor felt like big business, the companies that had a long history of strip-mining, clear-cutting, and creating pollution.

Those opposing such companies could find a resonance in Tolkien's books. As could the fledgling environmental movement. As could anyone who wished to preserve some of the natural beauty of the world, who might feel dismayed at the "progressive" concept that change is both necessary and good. I don't believe we were all Luddites. But we did want to see some balance struck between technological progress and more naturalistic values.

Am I reading too much into a simple pair of fantasy novels? I don't think so. But at the time, I also don't think that we were necessarily examining the reasons that Tolkien's books touched us the way they did. We allowed them into our lives, we were enriched by them on many levels, but we didn't feel the need to understand why. We were able to appreciate them as wonderful stories that also resonated to the way we felt about the world.

Perhaps the best reason for such appreciation can be found in Tolkien's own essay, "On Fairy-stories" (*Tree and Leaf,* 1964):

> Fantasy is a natural human activity. It certainly does not destroy or even insult Reason; and it does not either blunt the appetite for, nor obscure the perception of, scientific veracity. On the contrary. The keener and clearer the reason, the better fantasy it will make. If men were ever in a state in which they did not want to know or could not perceive truth (facts or evidence), then Fantasy would languish until they were cured. If they ever get into that state (it would not seem at all impossible), Fantasy would perish, and become Morbid Delusion.

While the cult of appreciation that sprang up in the wake of the publication of Tolkien's books certainly had its moments of being much too far over the top (remember graffiti written in runes or elvish script, or simply stating "Gandalf Lives!"?), such rabid fans were a minority. There were many other readers who had a quieter and more personal relationship with the books. They understood what Tolkien was getting at in the above quote, that there needs to be a balance between fantasy and reality, how our lives are so much the poorer when the balance becomes uneven—no matter which way it leans.

The Hobbit, and especially The Lord of the Rings, went on to influence generations of young writers, myself being included in the second or third wave. Some us wrote lavish imitations and continue to do so. Some of us began by writing such imitations, but then went looking for our own voices. How many of us would be writers today without Tolkien's direct or indirect influence, how large an audience for fantasy there would be without the genre he inadvertently created, is hard to say. But frankly, for all the misuse of the tools he popularized and then put in our hands, I still think the world would be a much dimmer place without his gift of Middle-earth.

And the most telling thing is how these books are still so powerful today, easily rising above the crowds of crass imitators and heartfelt tributes with which they share the shelves of libraries and bookstores. Yes, it would have been nice if Tolkien could have had some more strong, well-drawn female characters (though to be fair, how much would a cloistered Oxford don know about such exotic—to him—creatures?). And surely a world as large and diverse as Middle-earth would have been strongly influenced by religion in some form or another.

Yet even such critiques wither before the books themselves—the Story, the wealth of detail, the characters that we are given in its pages.

I can still enjoy these books, and I don't believe my pleasure is nostalgic. And I don't believe I'm alone, either. Tolkien might have passed on, but the words remain. And, to paraphrase "The Road Goes Ever On" (the title song from Donald Swann's folio of Tolkien lyrics set to music back in 1967), the tale goes ever on.

THE MYTH-MAKER

MAKER

LISA GOLDSTEIN

I first read J. R. R. Tolkien in the eighth grade, when a classmate of mine gave a book report on The Lord of the Rings. I was impressed by her passion, by her clear delight in the book, and so—despite the fact that she gave away the ending—I borrowed a copy of *The Fellowship of the Ring* from a friend. (I have remembered the name of the girl who gave the book report from that day to this, and if I ever meet her again I mean to have words with her about giving away that ending.)

My friend was still working on the second volume when I finished the first. I was distraught. What had happened to Gandalf? I ran to the corner drugstore and got *The Two Towers*. This remains fixed in my mind as one of the first times I ever bought a book.

I ended up reading the series every year of my adolescence. I read it until those first paperbacks wore out; I read it until I practically had it memorized, and—unfortunately—could not look at it again for a long while, having become familiar with every twist and turn, every poetic phrase.

I learned later that I wasn't the only one to do this. I even read a book once where, to demonstrate what a nerd one of the characters was, the author mentions that the character read The Lord of the Rings every year. Okay, so we're nerds. I made myself a cloak once; I even went out with a guy who called himself Bilbo. Guilty. But what the author of this book—I can't remember the title, but it was mainstream, obviously—failed to understand is how powerful The Lord of the Rings actually is.

The question, though, is why. Why do people read and reread these books? Why are they so powerful? What do we get from them that we can't get anywhere else? How did one man working alone manage to call into being an entire genre, an entire publishing industry?

My guess is that it's because we need myth. Not just because myths are entertaining stories, or because some of them come attached with a moral. We *need* them, the way we need vitamins or sunlight.

I read The Lord of the Rings at the tail end of the sixties, when it seemed that everyone was busily searching for a myth, a religion, a way to make some kind of meaning out of their world. My school was overrun with kids carrying the Bible, or books by Alan Watts, or Chairman Mao's little red book. There was a sense that our parents had failed us somehow, that we had missed something, that there was a larger world out there we had never been told about.

We had grown up in the fifties; our parents had survived the Depression and the horrors of World War II, and now just wanted to make a life for themselves in the midst of America's new prosperity. Not for them the troubling questions about myth and meaning, the dragons slithering up from the psyche. Fairy tales became comfortable stories told to children; the dwarfs of *Snow White* were no longer mysterious and sometimes frightening earth-dwellers, but cute little men named Grumpy and Sneezy. Even religion became something we thought about for a few days each year and forgot the rest of the time.

The idea was that science had triumphed, that we lived in an Age of Science. Diseases that had terrified people for centuries had been nearly wiped out; nuclear power was about to give us unlimited sources of energy.

The Age of Science certainly brought a lot of benefits—I'm not saying that smallpox and polio were good things. But somehow the idea grew that science and myth could not coexist, that myth was the same as superstition, and had to be suppressed. And I think this loss of myth was one of the reasons my generation searched so hard and went, some of them, down such disastrous paths.

Myths had started their decline long before the fifties,

though. Tolkien himself, in his famous essay "On Fairy-stories," puts the beginning somewhere around the Elizabethan Age. Once upon a time, fairies had been called the Fair Folk to placate them, and people thought of them as capricious and unpredictable, beautiful and terrifying, anything but fair. But in the works of Michael Drayton and Shakespeare himself, they became tiny, dainty, merely pretty. They lost their power to astonish and frighten; they dwindled, both in stature and importance. They became a subject for children and, eventually, as Tolkien puts it, were "relegated to the nursery."

Not surprisingly, this happened at about the same time that people were beginning to understand certain things about their world, were beginning to experiment, were starting on the road that would take them from alchemy to chemistry, from astrology to astronomy.

The need for myth became especially acute after World War I, when all the certainties of the old values were swept away, when, not coincidentally, Tolkien began his tale. Part of his genius was that he realized this hunger still existed, despite all the marvels of the modern world. He knew that people need epic stories of journeys, dragons, treasure, magic, wonders, terrors, loss, and redemption, of heroes stretched nearly beyond their capacity for endurance. We need them because they're magnificent stories, of course, tales that have been told as long as people existed. But we also need them because they are stories about the hero who journeys into a dark place and comes out transformed, and that is a story we all know intimately, a story each of us experiences in his or her life. Those dragons are our dragons, those magical helpers our helpers. And sometimes the dragons are inside us, a part of us, and this is the most terrifying struggle of all. No wonder an entire generation wanted nothing to do with myth.

If that was all, we'd probably never have heard of this man Tolkien. But his genius also showed itself in the way he was able to satisfy that hunger. Working in the twentieth century, at a time of cars and airplanes and radios, he revived an old form and somehow made it speak to the present. He spent, literally, decades constructing his world, making it consistent, giving it languages and poetry and history and art, making it so real we might believe that he had discovered it rather than invented it. He gave it characters of stature—metaphorical if not literal—people who fit the grandeur of the place. And he set in motion a story that we read again and again.

How did he do it? How was he able to write an epic in a time when epics were all but forgotten? How did he tap into the collective unconscious of so many people? I don't know. Sorry. You might check Joseph Campbell's *The Hero with a Thousand Faces,* another response to the lack of myth in the twentieth century. Campbell gives a template for the hero's journey, from the Call to Adventure to the Descent into Darkness—the Night-sea Journey—and finally the Emergence of the Hero Reborn, and you might note that there are at least three of these descents in The Lord of the Rings: Gandalf in Moria, Frodo's and Sam's journey into Mordor, and Aragorn in the Paths of the Dead. But Tolkien, of course, didn't use a template—for one thing, The Lord of the Rings was nearly finished when Campbell's book came out. More importantly, the unconscious does not follow rules; it cannot be forced into a template.

Tolkien himself, in the introduction to The Lord of the Rings, says that he was writing a story "that would hold the attention of readers, amuse them, delight them, and at times maybe excite them or deeply move them. As a guide I had only my own feelings for what is appealing or moving. . . ." I think that's the closest we'll come to understanding how he did it. Somehow he went deep into his unconscious—another Descent into Darkness—went into the part of his mind where the stories come from, and he returned to the everyday world with this one. That's why he was a genius; there's really no explaining them.

There is one explanation for his success I can give, though, one small piece of the mystery I can illuminate. I think some of it has to do with language. An epic tale needs an epic voice, a poetic voice, a voice raised above the babble and trivia of the everyday world. There should be a hint of the ancient world in this voice, an understanding that the storyteller is dealing with a heroic age, with people who were, if not better than, *more* than us. (But only a hint. A little archaism can go a long way.)

Tolkien, a professor of languages and a connoisseur of words, knew all about this; so did Homer, and the author of *Beowulf,* and whoever wrote the more poetic parts of the Bible. He turned to these examples as he wrote, an achievement that is all the more impressive when you realize that he was writing in a time that worshiped Hemingway and his stripped-down, no-nonsense prose. (Geniuses, of course, pay no attention to fashions.) Listen to these lines, to the rhythms, to the spell he is weaving here:

CIRITH UNGOL

The Return of the King

Book 4, Chapter I: "The Tower of Cirith Ungol"

He [Frodo] stood as he had at times stood enchanted by fair elven-voices; but the spell that was now laid upon him was different: less keen and lofty was the delight, but deeper and nearer to mortal heart; marvellous and yet not strange. "Fair lady Goldberry!" he said again. "Now the joy that was hidden in the songs we heard is made plain to me."

The Fellowship of the Ring

"Gibbets and crows!" he [Saruman] hissed, and they shuddered at the hideous change. "Dotard! What is the house of Eorl but a thatched barn where brigands drink in the reek, and their brats roll on the floor among the dogs? Too long have they escaped the gibbet themselves. But the noose comes, slow in the drawing, tight and hard in the end. Hang if you will!"

The Two Towers

"Begone, foul dwimmerlaik, lord of carrion! Leave the dead in peace."

A cold voice answered: "Come not between the Nazgûl and his prey! Or he will not slay thee in thy turn. He will bear thee away to the houses of lamentation, beyond all darkness, where thy flesh shall be devoured, and thy shrivelled mind be left naked to the Lidless Eye."

A sword rang as it was drawn. "Do what you will; but I will hinder it, if I may."

"Hinder me? Thou fool. No living man may hinder me!"

Then Merry heard of all sounds in that hour the

strangest. It seemed that Dernhelm laughed, and the clear voice was like the ring of steel. . . .

The Return of the King

If none of that makes you shiver, you might be dead.

The first example describes a small part of the beauty of Middle-earth, the other two its terror. (Tolkien, unlike many writers, was adept at both.) And I wasn't joking about these pieces making you shiver. The last is especially shiver-inducing to me, a description of heroism against all odds, of triumph, made even sweeter because it is about one of Tolkien's few female characters. You don't even have to know what "dwimmerlaik" means; it's one of those archaisms I talked about earlier, an authentic reminder that we are in another time, another place. By the sound of it (say it out loud), and in context, we understand that it means something foul, something terrifying.

But, you say, there have been many followers of Tolkien, some who slavishly imitated him, and some who went their own way, and these people do not use poetic language. Sometimes the opposite, in fact; sometimes the ineptness of their writing can make you wince. I haven't kept up with all the writers of epic fantasy—I don't think anyone can, these days—but the only ones I know of who understand the importance of language are Ursula Le Guin, Patricia McKillip, and Greer Gilman. (Le Guin even wrote a wonderful essay on this subject, called "From Elfland to Poughkeepsie.") This is a matter very near and dear to my heart, so I hope you will permit me a small rant here.

(But first, a digression. There are some books that are marketed as epic fantasy but are in fact histories, though histories of imaginary places. These have little or no magic, and are concerned with the stuff of history, intrigues and invasions and the like. They are, and should be, written in the language of history. So I can read Guy Gavriel Kay's novels with pleasure and without ranting—much to the relief of my husband, who's heard the rant a few times too many—and I'm having a very good time with George R. R. Martin's series.)

After I read The Lord of the Rings, I looked around for more of the same. At the time there seemed to be very little that provided the same thrill: some children's books, the Earthsea series, Lin Carter's amazing Ballantine Adult Fantasy series. Finally, at the end of the seventies, a number of books came out that were strongly influenced by The Lord of the Rings.

"Strongly influenced" may be understatement; there are scenes in at least one of these that seem to have been lifted in whole from Tolkien. I was working in a bookstore when this book came out, and I was very excited at the advanced publicity. As I said, I was starved for fantasy, and there are only so many times you can reread Tolkien. We ordered a display, what publishers call a "dump" (which gives you some idea of how publishers feel toward their books), containing, I think, eighteen copies. I got an advanced reading copy, settled down to be enchanted, and found myself reading a pale imitation of The Lord of the Rings.

I once felt very bitter toward this book; I thought (and still think, somewhat), that it is at least partly to blame for all the cheap tripe that came later. Now, though, I have a different view, a view I incline to in my less cynical moments. A myth is a story of a hero's journey into darkness, and his or her return. All myths are the same in this way; it is only the trappings that are different. Perhaps the author of this book, like all of us, was moved by this story, and moved to retell it; perhaps in retelling it he was more like a bard of old, singing a story he had heard to a transfixed audience around a fire. Myths were once told and retold, changed and rechanged; intellectual property is a fairly recent concept. That he proved to be such a poor bard compared to the master does not change the nature of the tale.

But when I read my advanced copy I despaired, and not just because I thought the book was derivative and the language clunky. I feared that no one would buy this thing, that we had ordered far too many copies and that they would all have to be returned, with us paying the postage on what was, after all, a fairly hefty tome (though nothing like the toe-crushers that followed). The bookstore had just opened, and a little thing like postage was a huge expense in those days.

To my absolute surprise, the book began to sell, and sold without ceasing. We got rid of the entire dump and had to pick up more copies at our local book distributor. I was in a bit of a quandary, though, when our customers asked me if it was any good, and ended up saying something like, "If one of the things you enjoyed about Tolkien was his language, you won't like this. But if you read Tolkien only for the story, you will find this very much like that, maybe too much so." To a man and a woman, they bought the book.

Then the floodgates opened. Hundreds of epic fantasies,

maybe even thousands, have been published since then. People realized that they could write them without paying attention to style, that they didn't have to spend decades building a world, but could make one out of cheap cardboard, or, even simpler, could borrow it from a better writer. Some of these books were so bad they wouldn't even make decent landfill. And these, too, were bought and eagerly devoured.

It's the story: the story is the important thing. People are so hungry for these tales that they will read them and make them best-sellers no matter how badly written they are. Some of them are poor retellings, but such is the power of the hero's journey that people will read them anyway. Even Hollywood has gotten into the act. Because of the success of *Star Wars*, which was inspired in part by *The Hero with a Thousand Faces*, you can hear Armani-suited, sunglass-wearing, cell-phone-toting producers talk with straight faces about the hero's journey. Or, as someone I know who works there said, "If I have to hear Joseph Campbell's name in this town one more time . . ."

So am I wrong about epic language? I still don't think so, though I admit to being crochety about the subject. People *do* enjoy a well-written book, even if they don't realize why they are getting that bit of extra enjoyment at the time. (A sort of subliminal suggestion, you might say.) More importantly, though, how many of these recent fantasies will stand the test of time? How many will people be reading a hundred years from now?

Very few, I think. But if the twenty-second century has any taste at all, they will still be reading Tolkien. They will marvel at his gift for storytelling, his solidly constructed world, his understanding of beauty and terror. And at his language. That language is one of the things that make him a true mythmaker. We have had precious few mythmakers in our time, and we should honor him. I'm glad we are.

"The Radical Distinction . . ."

A Conversation with Tim and Greg Hildebrandt

⟁⟁

Glenn Hurdling

Tim: It was 1967, so I was twenty-eight. Greg and I were making films on world hunger for Bishop Fulton J. Sheen for the Society of the Propagation of the Faith in New York City. I had done a watercolor painting of a dwarf skipping over a bridge by a tree when a girl in the office—her name was Winifred Boyle—saw it and said that it reminded her of Tolkien. I said, "What's a Tolkien?"

The next day she handed me *The Hobbit*. I was totally hooked the moment I began to read it. I devoured The Lord of the Rings next. I had never read anything like it in my life—before or after. To me, it is still the alpha and the omega of the fantasy genre.

Vivid pictures would pop into my head every time I turned a page. Greg and I weren't illustrators yet, so the possibility of illustrating the The Lord of the Rings seemed a bit absurd. But something about the thought stuck in my head, and I said, "I've got to paint this some day."

Then we got into illustrating, and one thing led to another. On Christmas morning, 1974, my wife Rita gave me the 1975 Tolkien Calendar, illustrated by Tim Kirk. A blurb on the back of the calendar announced that Ballantine Books was seeking new artists to illustrate the following year's calendar. I leaped out of my slippers.

I began to spend most of my free time painting castles and gnarled trees, always with Tolkien in the back of my mind.

Greg: I didn't read the books until 1975, despite Tim's insistence that I do so over the years. Up till then we had been doing illustrations for kids' books—for Disney and Sesame Street, panda and hippopotamus books for Golden Books, and even a book on toilet training! None of these things had any bearing on fantasy whatsoever. But at least by then we had become illustrators. We weren't necessarily doing the subject matter we wanted to do, but we were making a living doing what we did best.

I had been concentrating on painting my own images, with dreams of having my own gallery show in New York

City. I wanted to break away from illustrating someone else's ideas, so I had no desire to read The Lord of the Rings at all.

When Tim showed me the announcement on the back of that calendar, I put my desire for a gallery show on hold. I realized that I had a family to feed, so I finally gave in and read the trilogy. I was blown away! For the next three years, I immersed myself in a world of hobbits, wizards, dwarves, and elves.

Tim: We started to do sample sketches to show Ballantine right after I showed Greg the announcement. After a month and a half of sketching, we headed into New York. We didn't have a portfolio big enough to put any of our sample character sketches into, so we put them into these big green garbage bags. We brought them in expecting to get an appointment with the art director at Ballantine. We hung around all day and badgered the receptionist until we finally got to see Ian Summers, Ballantine's art director.

Very few people had illustrated Tolkien up to that point. Ian said that he had looked at a lot of samples, but they had all been submitted by amateurs, kids in school, or fans who scribbled their interpretations of the characters without illustrating any of the classic scenes. No professional artists had come forward except Greg and me. Can you imagine how many remarkable artists would be lined up around the block if a publisher made that announcement today? The line would be a mile long!

Greg: Tim and I had always read the same things growing up—Edgar Rice Burroughs' Pelucidar stuff, all of H. G.

Wells, most of Jules Verne, and Jack London. We also loved comic books and comic strips, such as *Prince Valiant*. But other than that, we weren't big readers. We were into the visual stuff; we taught ourselves painting and animation by watching Disney films and 1950s science-fiction films. We also loved medieval films, the ones with the cheesy swords and cardboard-aluminum armor. Robert Wagner and James Mason starred in a screen version of *Prince Valiant* that was quite exceptional. The scene in which Vikings attack the castle was one of our inspirations for "The Siege of Minas Tirith" in the 1977 Tolkien Calendar.

Tim: When we were kids, we believed in flying saucers. We would sit in the basement and create Martians. We also blew up model buildings in my parents' barn and filmed the blaze with our 8mm movie camera.

Greg: People thought we were pyromaniacs. And who could blame them? We'd spend a year building a model set, then blow it up!

Tim: I know our relatives thought we were strange. Our Aunt Gertie believed that we had an idol of Disney in our bedroom and that we burned a candle in front of it every night.

Greg: With the exception of our parents, our family didn't get the idea of special effects or visual expression. But we were completely freaked out over Disney and science fiction. *Rocket Ship X-M* was the first science-fiction film we ever saw, then *The Man from Planet X*.

Tim: That was all visual stimulation, but Tolkien's work resided in the imagination. I read *The Hobbit* and The Lord of the Rings four times each, and doing so painted good images in my imagination. We wanted to do justice to the books when we illustrated them by paying attention to all of Tolkien's detailed descriptions.

Greg: Well, not completely. For instance, Tolkien described Gandalf as having "long bushy eyebrows that stuck out further than the brim of his shady hat." If you read that, it's one thing; but try to paint it and it looks as goofy as hell.

Tim: You wouldn't even do that in a cartoon.

Greg: And there's nothing in the books about pointed ears on hobbits. Tolkien said they have "sharp ears," but nowhere does he say they're pointed. That was our own visual interpretation.

Tim: When I read *The Hobbit* the first time, the immediate visual imagery that came to me was of a rabbit character— the name "hobbit," the furry feet. I think Tolkien made the same analogy, too, when he created the creatures—tiny creatures who live in holes. So we tried to extend that imagery to the ears.

Greg: There was a debate with Lester Del Rey over the pointed ears; he was the consultant on our calendars. He had a business card that read "expert." I remember coming in with the painting of Faramir, whose arrow feathers we

EOWYN

The Return of the King

Chapter 6: "The Battle of Pelennor Fields"

had painted red. Lester said, "Uh-uh. Green. *The Two Towers,* page 336, paragraph 3." He debated whether our hobbits should have pointed ears, but he finally gave in. We did the painting of Bilbo, retired at Rivendell, and we put sideburns on him. There was a big discussion about whether hobbits could grow facial hair. But Lester agreed that we could bring the sideburns down into his face as an old man.

The pointed ears on elves, on the other hand, were a traditional interpretation. We gave Legolas blond hair, even though in the book he has dark hair. In *The Fellowship of the Ring* centerpiece of the first calendar, we painted him with blond hair and dressed him in light colors. Lester looked at it and said, "No, he has dark hair . . . but leave it!"

Tim: We generally stuck pretty close to the colors that Tolkien described. In *The Hobbit* it says that hobbits dress in bright colors—chiefly green and yellow. But I don't think they'd be wearing those colors if they were going on a dangerous quest. Why would they want to call attention to themselves if they were going to destroy an object of power in the far-off Cracks of Doom?

Greg: Their party clothes would be brightly colored.

Tim: I can see them wearing bright colors at parties, like that big party at the beginning of *The Fellowship of the Ring*.

Greg: Their disco look.

Tim: Gold buttons, green vests. They probably looked more like leprechauns, really.

Tolkien was never a big supporter of illustration to accompany works of fantasy. In his essay, "On Fairy-stories," Tolkien said, "However good in themselves, illustrations do little good to fairy-stories. The radical distinction between all art (including drama) that offers a *visible* presentation and true literature is that it imposes one visible form. Literature works from mind to mind and is thus more progenitive."

I can see where he's coming from, and I agree to a certain extent. The final piece can never look in reality as it does in your mind.

Greg: I guess Tolkien and Robert Louis Stevenson would have disagreed. Stevenson was a big, big supporter of visual imagery. He loved illustrations in his books, and he would build his stories to a big visual climax in his writing. He thought in terms of an illustrator. I understand Tolkien's point of view: you build up an image in your own head. But the challenge and the risk of being an illustrator is taking on an author's work and doing your take on it, hoping that it hits a soft spot with the fans of the book.

Tim: Tolkien was something of a frustrated illustrator himself. You could see it in his prose descriptions, as he tried to nail down those scenes to the minutest detail. I can't get into the guy's head . . . and I wouldn't want to!

Greg: I doubt that our representation of Tolkien's world would have succeeded for him.

Tim: But if we were to start all over again, there are certain things we would do totally differently today. For instance, the Rivendell painting in the 1977 Tolkien Calendar now looks too Disneyesque to me—it looks like Pinocchio's house or the Seven Dwarfs' house or something. Today we'd make it much more elaborate and imposing—more like an art nouveau, art deco combination with Frank Lloyd-Wright.

We'd probably also make the Balrog in the 1977 Calendar more like Tolkien described it. It would look pretty cool with flames coming off it.

Greg: The thing is, when you read the Balrog passage, it's really just a dark shape surrounded by flame. So we compromised in order to "solidify" the figure. Right, wrong, or indifferent, good or bad, that's what we did. We really couldn't depict it the way it was described because it was just a dark shadow—like many of Tolkien's evildoers—surrounded by flame. We had to make it a three-dimensional solid figure standing in front of Gandalf. The description was kind of vague—wings, a mane of fire.

But Lester never disagreed with our interpretation of the Balrog. It was a great time, because the people at Ballantine pretty much let us do our own thing, which, in retrospect, was really pretty amazing.

Tim: The Lord of the Rings was already established as a cult phenomenon, and was experiencing a second-generation renaissance. Remember in the New York subways—"Frodo lives!"? Initial fan reaction to the calendar was exceptional. It was huge—it overwhelmed us.

Greg: If Ballantine received any negative letters, we never saw them. For the most part, people were in sync with our interpretation.

Tim: All the letters we received expressed pretty much the same thing: "You painted it just the way I imagined it!"

Greg: That's what we've heard more than anything over the years. Our fans keep asking if we'll ever collect into one book every Tolkien-related illustration we've ever created. We've finally put one together called *Greg and Tim Hildebrandt: The Tolkien Years* (Watson-Guptill, 2001). It not only contains all of our original paintings, but some never-before-published ones as well. We also just painted a cover for the book, and a centerfold based on photos we took in 1977 for what would have been the fourth Tolkien calendar. So I guess you *can* go home again.

Tim: The centerfold is a rendition of "The Siege of Minas Tirith." The painting that appeared in the 1977 Tolkien Calendar was originally planned to be a much larger depiction of the dramatic battle. But due to looming deadline pressures, we were forced to scale down the painting to the version that saw print. Now we finally had the chance to do it right!

Greg: We shifted the camera angle a bit, and threw a whole bunch of stuff into the painting.

Tim: There are orcs, elves, armies, and oliphaunts, all surrounded by walls of flame. Like I said, there's no literal interpretation of the subject matter, but it's as if there's some spirit there that overtakes us when we do this stuff.

Greg: I remember approaching the original material with total artistic integrity, putting ourselves completely into the scene and seeing the reality of that world.

Tim: Hal Foster, Walt Disney, *Pinocchio*—all the visual stimulation that inspired us as kids now had a vessel in which to launch.

Greg: By the third calendar, we had decided that The Lord of the Rings should be a live-action movie, and we should be its art directors. So we assembled a lot of the art and started to shoot it. We showed Ian Summers our proposal, but he told us that Ralph Bakshi already had the rights to it. So we dropped it.

We decided that we'd do our own thing, but we had to make sure that it could be done as a movie. That was how we started *Urshurak*. We were projecting a film that we wanted to make, but Ian Summers insisted that it first had to be done as a book.

Tim: Urshurak was our epic fantasy quest. We felt that the trilogy lacked certain qualities for a modern movie audience. So we put a mingling of races and different cultures into our own story.

Greg: And heroic women took the spotlight. There were very few in Tolkien's work. What were there, three—maybe four—only one gets in on the action, disguised as a man! That was a big issue for us.

Tim: We conceived *Urshurak* visually because we wrote it by doing storyboards like they do for animation. We would draw actual floor plans of the buildings in which the action took place.

We like to think that our world was as visually complete in our minds as Tolkien's Middle-earth was structurally complete in his. We created maps, graphs, time charts, as well as different styles of architecture for the different realms in *Urshurak*.

Greg: At a presentation to the William Morris Agency in 1978, film producer Joseph E. Levine applauded our presentation but told us it would cost $145 million to produce. Even with special-effects genius John Dykstra onboard, we couldn't sell the project. But we're still proud of the book and of Jerry Nichols' writing, because we did it first and foremost for ourselves. It's similar to the claim that Tolkien's success lies in the fact that he created his world first for himself and for others only afterward.

Tim: It's like our approach to painting. You have to satisfy yourself first and hope that other people will be just as satisfied.

Greg: Half of the artistic process is internal—what the artist puts into it. But the other half is external—how the audience reacts to it. That's what places Tolkien on the high pedestal of art and literature.

Tim: If I remember correctly, Tolkien had built his world long before he ever made a dime off it. He wasn't even thinking about getting it published. It was his buddy, C. S. Lewis, who urged him to send it to a publisher.

I know that if I weren't painting today, I probably wouldn't be alive—and I'm sure that's how Tolkien felt about writing.

Greg: Doing it mainly to satisfy yourself is the criterion of real art versus commercial art.

Tim: Commercial artists primarily must be concerned with the target audience's reaction.

Greg: Tolkien's work in particular presents an incredible opportunity for self-expression. There was a freedom of expression here that we didn't have up to this point.

Tim: Nobody told us what style to paint in or how they wanted it done. At Ballantine, they let us do what we wanted to do, and evidently they were very pleased with the result.

Greg: One of the things I remember clearly about working on the The Lord of the Rings was that there was no commercial sense about it at Ballantine. That's rare nowadays. Everyone there was involved in The Lord of the Rings because they loved it. And they left us alone because they could see that we were passionate about it, too. And that passion ignited a fire all across the world. The last calendar ultimately sold over a million copies, which was unheard of back then. Our calendars started a proliferation of calendars in the marketplace. Epic fantasy departments in bookstores also boomed as a result of Tolkien, and maybe our calendars had something to do with that. Many fans have told us that our calendars actually introduced them to The Lord of the Rings, not the other way around.

Tim: If that's true, then I consider it an honor, a deep honor to have enhanced the fanfare of Tolkien's Ring with our art. Let's face it, we were already successful illustrators when we dumped our green garbage bags at Ballantine. . . .

Greg: But the calendars gave us a fan following that we never had before. Prior to Tolkien, we were known professionally and commercially by art directors and publishers. But Tolkien brought us worldwide recognition. We received tons of fan mail from all over the globe.

Tim: We had never done pure fantasy-genre illustrations before. I feel that Tolkien's work stands at the summit of the fantasy genre. In my opinion, The Lord of the Rings is the best epic fantasy ever written. Not that I'm an authority on literature or anything, but you've got to go a long way to even come close to Tolkien's genius. Anyone trying to compete with Tolkien would have some mighty big shoes to fill.

Greg: This was an all-new genre of art that we had never considered exploring. Tolkien opened up a new world of possibilities for us as artists, which subsequently introduced us to other exciting possibilities, including the possibility of creating our own worlds.

Tim: Who had ever thought about "fantasy" as being serious art?

Greg: Tolkien's work inspired us to push ourselves, to develop a new style that we had never before approached. It was a style of light and color, which the world has come to know us for. And we didn't have to push hard—somehow the subject matter made it all come naturally for us. By illustrating Tolkien, I was really able to open up and explore the use of light and color.

Tim: Because that's what the story is all about—light versus dark. Before Tolkien, we were really limited in what we could do as far as children's book illustrations. We could either do realistic, anthropomorphic animals or just straight cartoons.

Greg: Tolkien allowed us to approach a fantasy world with a realistic interpretation, and to draw from some of our greatest inspirations: N. C. Wyeth, Howard Pyle, even Rembrandt, Caravaggio, Raphael, and Michelangelo!

Tim: Part of me wishes we could go back again.

Greg: If we did, we'd do it over, and we'd do it better! J. R. R. Tolkien deserves only the best.

ON TOLKIEN AND FAIRY-STORIES

TERRI WINDLING

"I propose to speak about fairy-stories," begins a famous essay by J. R. R. Tolkien; and I can do no better than to echo the good professor's words today. I propose to speak about fairy-stories, and why these stories mattered to Tolkien. And why such stories, including Tolkien's own fairy-stories, have mattered to me.

In 1938, Tolkien was still best known as an Oxford language scholar; his children's tale, *The Hobbit*, had only just been published the year before, and he'd barely begun the long years of work on his adult epic, The Lord of the Rings. That year, Tolkien composed his essay "On Fairy-stories" as an Andrew Lang Lecture, delivered at the University of St. Andrews (subsequently published in 1947.)[1] In this essay, Tolkien made a learned attempt to define the nature of fairy tales, examine theories of their origin, and refute the notion that magical stories are the special province of children. Essentially, he was arguing the case for his own future masterwork, restoring magical fiction to its place in the adult literary tradition.

The association of children and fairy-stories, Tolkien pointed out, was an accident of domestic history. He compared such tales to old tables and chairs that were banished to the nursery because adults no longer wanted them, nor cared if they were misused. Fairy tales, he noted, are not necessarily stories about fairies, but stories about Fairy, or Faerie: the twilight realm where fairies exist. Many fairy tales contain no such creatures at all; they are tales of magic and marvels, and of ordinary men and women whose lives are transformed by enchantment. He likens fairy-stories to a pot of soup into which mythology, romance, history, hagiography, folk tales, and literary creations have all been tossed together and left to simmer through the centuries. Each story-teller drips into this soup when writing or recounting magical tales—the best of which have slipped right back into the collective pot. Shakespeare added to the soup with *The Tempest* and *A Midsummer Night's Dream,*

1. In *Essays Presented to Charles Williams*, Oxford University Press, 1947.

as did Chaucer, Mallory, Spenser, Pope, Milton, Blake, Keats, Yeats, and numerous other writers whose works were never intended for children.

It was only in the nineteenth century that magical literature and art was pushed into the nursery—ironically, at a time when adult interest in them could not have been higher. Prior to this, ancient epics and myths held a central place in the literary arts, while their country cousins, folk and fairy tales, were told to young and old alike. When fairy tales moved from the oral to the literary tradition, they did so as adult stories. In the West, the earliest published tales we know come from sixteenth-century Italy: Giovan Francesco Straparola's *The Pleasant Nights* and Giambattista Basile's *The Pentamerone*. Both volumes were sophisticated works published for educated adults; the stories they contained were sensual, violent, and complex. In the old versions of *Sleeping Beauty*, for instance, the princess is wakened not by a chaste kiss, but by the twins she gives birth to after the prince has come, fornicated with her sleeping body, and left again. Another prince claims Snow White's dead body and locks himself away with it; his mother, complaining of the dead girl's smell, is relieved when she returns to life. Cinderella doesn't sit weeping in the cinders while talking bluebirds flutter around her; she is a clever, angry, feisty girl who seeks her own salvation. In the seventeenth century, fairy tales were taken up by the avante garde in France, particularly women authors who were barred from the French Academy. Parisian writers dressed up old peasant folk tales in fashionable silks and jewels, using fairy tales to slyly critique aristocratic life. (So popular was this art form that when the French stories were finally collected, they filled up forty-one volumes of a work called *Les Cabinet de Fées*.) In the late eighteenth and early nineteenth centuries, the German Romantics (Goethe, Tieck, Novalis, de la Motte Fouqué, etc.) created works with mystical themes inspired by myths and fairy tales, while their countrymen, the Brothers Grimm, prepared their famous, influential volume, *German Popular Stories*. Works by the German Romantics were highly popular in nineteenth-century England, and the first English translation of the Grimms' collection (in 1823) fanned the fire of Victorian interest in all things magical and fey.

Victorian England was inundated with fairies. They danced upon the ballet stage, pranced through elaborate theatrical productions, trooped through enormous paintings hung in Royal Academy exhibitions. The overwhelming public interest in fairies was largely a product of the Industrial Revolution and the social upheavals engendered by this new economy. As vast tracts of English countryside disappeared forever under mortar and brick, fairies took on a glow of nostalgia for a vanishing way of life. Just as interest in fairy lore reached its peak, a peculiar thing happened: fairy-stories began to find themselves moved from the parlor to the childrens' rooms. There were two primary reasons for the sudden explosion of fairy books aimed at children. First, the Victorians romanticized the very idea of "childhood" to a degree that had not been known before—for earlier, it had not been viewed as something quite so separate and distinct from adult life. (Our modern notion of childhood as a special time for play and exploration is rooted in these Victorian ideals, although in the nineteenth century this held true only for the upper classes. Working-class children still labored long hours in the fields and factories, as Charles Dickens portrayed in his fiction—and as a child experienced himself.) The second reason was the growth of a new middle class that was both literate and wealthy. There was money to be made by exploiting the Victorian love affair with childhood; publishers had found a market, and they needed product with which to fill it. Cheap story material was available to them by plundering the fairy tales of other lands, simplifying them for young readers, then further editing the stories to conform to the rigid standards of the day—turning heroines into passive, modest, dutiful Victorian girls, and heroes into square-jawed fellows rewarded for their Christian virtues.

In his Andrew Lang Lecture (named for one of these very Victorian editors, although certainly not the worst of them), Tolkien decried this bowdlerization of the older fairy-story tradition. "Fairy-stories banished in this way, cut off from a full adult-art, would in the end be ruined; indeed, in so far as they have been so banished, they have been ruined." Tolkien would have been discouraged indeed had he known that worse was still to come, for Walt Disney would do more damage to the tales than all Victorian editors put together. Just the year before, Disney had released *Snow White*, his first feature-length cartoon, making sweeping changes to this story of a mother and daughter's poisonous relationship. Disney expanded the role of the prince, making the square-jawed fellow pivotal to the plot; he turned the dwarves into comically adorable (and thoroughly sexless) creatures. In this singing, dancing, whistling version, only the queen retains some of her old power. She's a genuinely frightening figure, and far more compelling than the giggling, simpering Snow White—who is introduced in Cinderella's rags, downtrodden but plucky. This gives Disney's rendition of the tale its peculiarly American flavor, implying that what we are watching is an Horatio Alger–type rags-to-riches story. (In fact, it's a story of riches to rags to riches, in which privilege is lost and then restored. Snow White's pedigree beauty and class origins, not her housekeeping skills, assure her salvation.) Although the film was a commercial triumph, and has been beloved by generations of children, critics through the years have protested the broad changes Disney Studios made, and continues to make, when retelling such tales. Walt himself responded, "It's just that people now don't want fairy stories the way they were written. They were too rough. In the end they'll probably remember the story the way we film it anyway." Regrettably, time has proved him right. Through films, books, toys, and merchandise recognized all around the world, Disney, not Tolkien, is the name most associated with fairy-stories today.

Disney, and the imitative books he spawned, bears a large part of the responsibility for our modern ideas about fairy tales and their fitness only for small children. And not all children at that, Tolkien argues persuasively in "On Fairy-Stories." Children, he says, cannot be considered a separate class of being with tastes all formed alike. Some children, like some adults, are born with a natural appetite for marvels, while other children, even those raised side by side, simply are not. Those of us born with this appetite usually find that it doesn't diminish with age, unless society teaches us to repress or sublimate it. Tolkien, of course, was the kind of child who hungered for marvels and magical adventures. "I desired dragons with a profound desire," he tells us eloquently. And yet, he notes, fairy tales had not been his only interest in childhood. There were many things that he liked just as much, or more: history, astronomy, botany, grammer, and etymology. A deeper passion for fairy-stories developed "on the threshold of manhood," where it was "wakened by philology." And, he adds almost as an aside, it was "quickened to full life by the war."

I desired dragons with a profound desire. Most Tolkien readers, I suspect, have felt that very same sentiment. I certainly did, and yet I, too, desired many other things as well; and music, not books, played a far more dominate role in my early years. A stronger interest in fairy-stories wakened, like Tolkien's, "on the threshold of adulthood," and was, like his, "quickened to life by war," of a peculiar sort. Before I leave the good green hills of Tolkien's England for my own America, I'd like to take a moment to look at war in relation to fairy-stories. Tolkien himself does not dwell on this subject in the text of his Andrew Lang Lecture, and yet (as Tolkien scholars have argued) the experience of a world at war, of evil that threatened the land he loved, informs every single page of Frodo's journey through Middle-earth. It is this—along with the elegant framework of myth and philology on which his tale is constructed—that lifts The Lord of the Rings from entertainment into literature.

Another great fantasist, Alan Garner,[2] has written about his own experience as a child in England during World War II, and how such experience affects the writing of magical fiction. "My wife," Garner notes, "claims to find, in recent

2. Author of *The Owl Service, Elidor, Red Shift, Strandloper*, and other fine books.

children's literature, little that qualifies as literature. She asked herself why this should be, after a Golden Age that ran from the late Fifties to the late Sixties. And she found that generally writers of this Golden Age were children during the Second World War: a war raged against civilians. The atmosphere these children and young people grew up in was one of a whole community and a whole nature united against pure evil, made manifest in the person of Hitler. Parents were seen to be afraid. Death was a constant possibility. . . . Therefore, daily life was lived on a mythic plane: of absolute Good against absolute Evil; of the need to endure, to survive whatever had to be overcome, to be tempered in whatever furnace was required. . . . Those children who were born writers, and would be adolescent when the full horrors [of the concentration camps] became known, would not be able to avoid concerning themselves with the issues; and so their books, however clad, were written on profound themes, and were literature. The generation that has followed is not so fueled, and its writing is, by comparison, effete and trivial."[3]

While I agree with Garner that the "tempering furnace" of war has resulted in fine works of fantasy, I'd like to suggest that mythic themes can be found in other areas of life—including the domestic sphere that has been the historical province of women. Let's take a look at the field of magical fiction published during the twentieth century, a field that, thanks to Tolkien, expanded rapidly from the sixties onward. It is possible to divide these books into two related but different kinds of tales: those rooted in the

3. In his essay collection *The Voice That Thunders*, The Harvill Press, 1998.

themes, symbols, and language of myth, epic, and romance, and those rooted in the humbler stuff of folklore and fairy tales. The first category includes tales epic in scope, full of sweeping heroic adventures and battles on which the fate of worlds, or at least kingdoms, depend. The later category includes much smaller tales, more intimate in nature—stories of individual rites of passage and personal transformation.[4] Historically, epic literature was composed by men of the privileged classes, and preserved by highly educated bards, monks, scholars, and publishers. The oral folk-tale tradition, on the other hand, was a peasant tradition, and a largely female one. Even its male literary proponents (Basile, Straparola, Perrault, and the Grimms) acknowledged that the bulk of their source material came from women storytellers. What interests me here is that Tolkien's clear preference for the first category was "quickened" by his experience of war in its most epic form: the great horrors of World War II. My own preference for the second category grew out of a different kind of war—an intimate war, a tempering furnace confined to the home front.

In the sixties, as Tolkien's hobbit and elves set sail across the wide Atlantic, I was a child growing up in an American working-class family. My stepfather was a truck driver, often unemployed, usually drunk; my mother held the family together working two, or three, or even four jobs at once, all of them menial, underpaid, demoralizing, and exhausting. Our small household was not unique, for this

4. Some authors write in both modes, of course. Tolkien himself adopted the fairy-tale voice in his shorter fiction.

was the industrial Northeast where the steelworks and the factories that had sustained the previous generations were now all closing down, one after another, and moving south. Another thing that was not unique was the daily violence in our home—violence that broke bones, left scars, and sent us children to the hospital, where jaded, overworked doctors (in those days before child abuse reporting laws) sutured and plastered and bandaged us up and sent us back home again. There was nothing remarkable in this. Neighborhood kids sported black eyes too; their fathers were also out of work. That these men were angry was something we all knew. That they were frightened is something I only later understood. In the world my stepfather had nothing, but at home he could rule as a king, and the one measure of manhood that he had left lay in his fists. My brothers and I didn't need Hitler's bombs to understand how Sauron came to be; we didn't need the Third Reich to make us feel helpless as hobbits.

It wasn't until I turned fourteen that I discovered Tolkien's books. I began *The Fellowship of the Ring* on the school bus sometime during that year, reading with pure amazement as Middle-earth opened up before me. Culture, back then, came largely from the radio and the television, where *The Brady Bunch* strained credulity far greater than any fairy-story. But here, *here*, in this fantasy book I found reality, and truth—for ours was a childhood in which good and evil were not abstract concepts. Here, the mortal battle between the two became a tangible thing. Darkness spread over Middle-earth, corrupting everything it touched, and yet our hero persevered, armed with the greatest magics of all: the loyalty of his friends and the courage of a noble

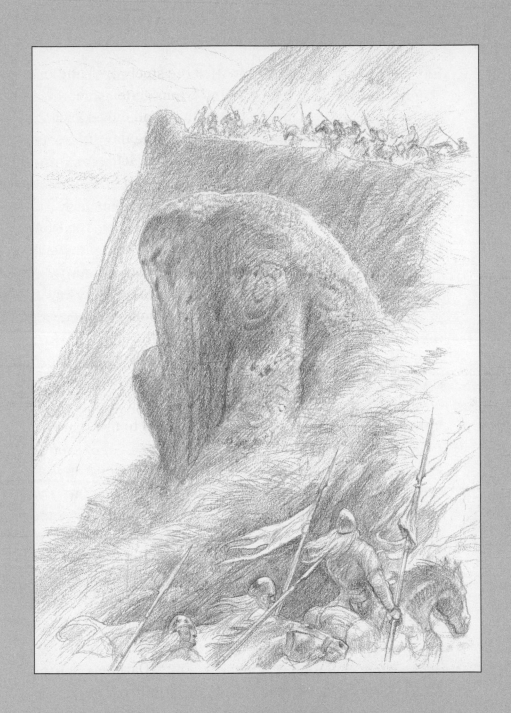

THE DUNKEL-MAN

The Return of the King

Chapter III: "The Muster of Rohan"

heart. I read Tolkien's great trilogy in one gulp, and was profoundly changed . . . not, I have to add, because those books truly satisfied me. What they did was to reawaken my taste for magic, my old *desire for dragons*. But even then, in the years before I quite understood what feminism was, I saw that there was no place for me, a girl, on Frodo's quest. Tolkien woke a longing in me . . . and then it was to other books I turned—to Mervyn Peake, E. R. Eddison, Lord Dunsany, and William Morris, searching through those magical kingdoms for a country where *I* could live.

Some months after I finished The Lord of the Rings, I discovered Tolkien's *Leaf by Niggle*, a volume containing the expanded text of his essay "On Fairy-stories." How, now, can I possibly convey the elation this slender book gave me? To understand, perhaps I must set the scene a bit more clearly. Picture a girl, rather small, quite bruised, frail of health and preternaturally quiet. Nights, at that particular time, when going home was problematic, I often spent in a secret nest I'd made (unbeknownst to anyone except a sympathetic janitor) in a hidden corner of the prop room behind my high school's auditorium stage. Terror and exhaustion have never been known as aids to education, and so it was with laborious effort that I made my way through Tolkien's prose, my critical faculties strained to their limit by this Oxfordian scholar. I didn't understand all of it, not then. But I knew, somehow, this essay was for me. "It was in fairy-stories," Tolkien told me, "that I first divined the potency of the words, and the wonder of the things, such as stone, and wood, and iron; tree and grass; house and fire; bread and wine." *Yes, yes, yes,* I murmured, excited now, for I'd felt that too. And this: "I desired dragons with a profound desire. Of course, I in my timid body did not wish to have them in the neighborhood . . . But the world that contained even the imagination of Fáfnir was richer and more beautiful, at whatever the cost of peril." And especially this: " . . . it is one of the lessons of fairy-stories (if we can speak of the lessons of things that do not lecture) that on callow, lumpish, and selfish youth peril, sorrow, and the shadow of death can bestow dignity, and even sometimes wisdom."

The thing that I took away from this essay, imperfectly as I understood it then, was that fairy tales had once been so much more than Disney cartoons. So I went back to the-fairy tale book that had been my favorite as a young child: *The Golden Book of Fairy Tales*, translated from the French by Marie Ponsot, and exquisitely, deliciously illustrated by Adrienne Segur. And here it was that I found at last the country that I could wander in, the water that would quench my thirst, and the food that would quell the ache in my belly. For I had been very fortunate as a child—this was no bowdlerized collection. These tales, largely taken from the Russian and the French, had been shortened for young readers but not simplified. Tolkien himself had never enjoyed the French tales of D'Aulnoy and Perrault, but I found in their rococo imagery exactly what I'd been looking for: intimate stories that spoke, in a coded language, of personal transformation. These were tales of children abandoned in woods; of daughters poisoned by their mothers' hands; of sons forced to betray their siblings; of men and women struck down by wolves, or imprisoned in window-less towers. I read of the girl who dared not speak if she wanted to save her swan-brothers from harm; I read, heart pounding, of Donkeyskin, whose own father desired to bed her. The tales that affected me the most were variations on one archetypal theme: a young person beset by grave difficulties sets off, alone, through the deep, dark woods, armed only with quick wits, clear sight, persistance, courage, and compassion. It is by these virtues we identify the heroes; it is with these tools that they make their way. Without these tools, no magic can save them. They are at the mercy of the wolf and wicked witch.

A year later, my own life reached the inevitable crisis of a classic fairy tale. I asked for a dress the color of the moon, the color of the sun, the color of the sky, but nothing I did kept evil at bay, and so I fled. Living on the streets of a distant city, my possessions fit into one small sack: two pairs of jeans; two flannel shirts; some letters from my first, lost love; a travel-stained sleeping bag; and *The Golden Book of Fairy Tales*. Like Frodo Baggins, I discovered I had the gift of making true friendships; and like the heroes of fairy tales, as I traveled onward through the woods, I learned that no kindness, however small, goes unrewarded. I learned how to tell friend from foe, and met helpers along the road, animal guides and fairies cloaked in the most unlikely disguises.

A year later, by magic as powerful as any enchanted ring, I found myself in the safe harbor of a small midwestern college. It was here that I discovered the legacy J. R. R. Tolkien had left behind: a whole new publishing genre called *fantasy*, rooted in myth and magic. It was deeply important to me that some of these books were written by women authors: Ursula Le Guin, Patricia A. McKillip, Joy Chant, Susan Cooper, C. L. Moore, and many others, blazing trails into the lands where I longed to make my home. I studied literature, folklore, and women's studies, and satisfied my hunger with the scholarly works of Katherine Briggs, the fiction of Sylvia Townsend Warner and Angela Carter, the fairy-tale poetry of Anne Sexton, the fairy-tale art of Jessie M. King . . . all of which proved that Tolkien had been right: fairy-stories could rise to Art. And that even I, a working-class girl, could add to the soup of story.

College, for me, marked my emergence from the dark woods to a brighter place, the fertile lands where life could now be lived *happily ever after*. This does not mean, of course, a life free of difficulties and challenges, but one that partakes of the qualities that Tolkien required in a fairy-story's ending: the consolation of joy and what he called "a miraculous grace." As fond as I am of this brighter land, there are times when I journey back into those woods, back into the dark, back *once upon a time* into the endless story. Now, however, I have a different part to play. I'm not the hero struggling through; I'm the one waiting by the side of the road, disguised, and ready to the light the way for those who come behind me.

Wherever I stand waiting on that road, Tolkien has usually been there before. If I ever come face to face with him in that forest, I shall shake his hand.

ABOUT THE AUTHORS

Karen Haber is the author of eight novels including *Star Trek Voyager: Bless the Beasts* (Pocket Books) and a three-book series for Daw Books, *Woman Without a Shadow, The War Minstrels,* and *Sister Blood*. She is co-author of *Science of the X-Men*. Her short fiction has appeared in *Isaac Asimov's Science Fiction Magazine, The Magazine of Fantasy and Science Fiction,* and many anthologies, including *Sandman: Book of Dreams* and *Alien Pets*. She lives in Oakland, California.

George R. R. Martin is the award-winning author of five novels, including *Fever Dream* and *The Armageddon Rag*. For the last ten years, he has been a screenwriter for feature films and television and was the producer of the TV series *Beauty and the Beast* as well as a story editor for *The Twilight Zone*. After a ten-year hiatus, he has now returned to writing novels full-time and is presently at work on *A Dance with Dragons,* the fourth book of his Song of Ice and Fire series.

Raymond E. Feist's latest book, *Krondor the Asssassins,* is the second book of his Riftwar Legacy series, following on the heels of *Krondor, the Betrayal*. His previous novels include *Magician, Silverthron, Faerie Tale, Prince of the Blood,* and *The King's Buccanner,* as well as the four books of his *New York Times* bestselling Serpentwar Saga. He is the creator of the immensely popular computer game *Betrayal at Krondor*—which won *Computer Magazine*'s Best Game of the Year Award—and the follow-up game, *Return to Krondor*.

Poul Anderson was born in the United States of Scandinavian parents, hence the spelling of his first name. He majored in physics at the University of Minnesota, then went into freelance writing. In 1953 he moved to the San Francisco Bay Area and married Karen Kruse, with whom he worked in close consultations and sometimes collaboration. Their daughter Astrid is married to their colleague Greg Bear and has given them two grandchildren. Anderson is best known in the science fiction and fantasy fields and had received numerous honors, including seven Hugos, four

Nebulas, the J. R. R. Tolkien Memorial Award, and the Grand Master Award of the Science Fiction and Fantasy Writers of America. Among his fantasy works are *The Broken Sword, Three Hearts and Three Lions, Hrolf Kraki's Saga, The Merman's Children, The King of Ys* (with Karen Anderson), *Operation Chaos,* and *Operation Luna.* Forthcoming is *Mother of Kings.* He passed away on July 31, 2001.

Michael Swanwick has received the Hugo Award for best science fiction short story in both 1999 and 2000, in addition to previous Nebula, Theodore Sturgeon, and World Fantasy Awards. He is the author of five novels and sixty short stories, all science fiction or fantasy. His most recent novel, *Jack Faust,* was published by Avon. He had two short story collections published in 2000: *Moon Dogs,* and *Tales of Old Earth.* A new novel, tentatively titled *A Feast of Dinosaurs*, will be published by HarperCollins in 2002. He lives in Philadelphia with his wife, Marianne Porter, and their son, Sean.

Esther Friesner is the author of twenty-nine novels and over one hundred short stories, in addition to being the editor of six popular anthologies. Her works have been published in the United States, the United Kingdom, Japan, Germany, Russia, France, and Italy. Her articles on fiction writing have appeared in *Writer's Market* and *Writer's Digest Books*. Besides winning two Nebula Awards in succession for Best Short Story (1995 and 1996, from the Science Fiction Writers of America), she was a Nebula finalist twice and a Hugo finalist once. She received the Skylark Award from NESFA and the award for Most Promising New Fantasy Writer of 1986 from *Romantic Times*. She lives in Connecticut with her husband, two children, two rambunctious cats, and a fluctuating population of hamsters.

Harry Turtledove was born in Los Angeles in 1949. After flunking out of Caltech, he earned a Ph.D. in Byzantine history from UCLA. He has taught ancient and medieval history at UCLA, Cal State Fullerton, and Cal State L.A., and has published a translation of a ninth-century Byzantine chronicle and several scholarly articles. He is also a full-time science fiction and fantasy writer; much of his work involves either alternate histories or historically based fantasy. Most recent releases include *Colonization: Down to Earth*, which continues the universe established in the Worldwar books, and *Darkness Descending*, a high-tech fantasy, also the second in a series. His alternate-history novella, *Down in the Bottom-*

lands, won the 1994 Hugo award in its category. An alternate-history novelette, "Must and Shall," was a 1996 Hugo and 1997 Nebula finalist. "Forty, Counting Down" was a 2000 Hugo finalist. He is married to fellow novelist Laura Frankos Turtledove. They have three daughters, Alison, Rachel, and Rebecca.

Terry Pratchett's acclaimed Discworld novels have topped the bestseller lists in England for more than a decade, and sold more than twenty million copies worldwide. Pratchett's unique brand of irreverent satirical humor has placed him in the pantheon of the most celebrated practitioners of literary parody around the globe.

Robin Hobb is the author of the Farseer Trilogy (*Assassin's Apprentice, Royal Assassin,* and *Assassin's Quest*) and the Liveship Traders Trilogy (*Ship of Magic, Mad Ship,* and *Ship of Destiny*). She is currently at work on The Tawny Man. Book one is titled *Fool's Errand,* and will see print in January or February of 2002. She resides in Tacoma, Washington. For more information, see the Hobb website at http://robinhobbonline.com.

Ursula K. Le Guin has published over eighty short stories, two collections of essays, ten books for children, several volumes of poetry, and sixteen novels, including the Earthsea Trilogy, *The Lathe of Heaven,* and *The Left Hand of Darkness.* Among the honors her writing has received are a National Book Award, five Hugo and four Nebula Awards, the Kafka Award, a Pushcart Prize, and the Howard Vursell Award of the American Academy of Arts and Letters. She lives in Portland, Oregon.

Diane Duane is the author of over two dozen novels of science fiction and fantasy, among them the *New York Times* bestsellers *Spock's World* and *Dark Mirror,* her popular Wizard fantasy series, and *Venom Factor,* a Spider-Man hardcover novel, plus other novels set in the *Star Trek* universe. She lives with her husband, Peter Morwood—with whom she has written five novels including *New York Times* bestseller *The Romulan Way*—in a valley in rural Ireland.

Douglas A. Anderson published his first book, *The Annotated Hobbit,* in 1988. He corrected text in The Lord of the Rings in both the American and English editions, and both versions contain his introductory "Note on the Text" (U.S. edition, 1987; U.K. edition, 1994). He is also the co-author (with Wayne G. Hammond) of *J. R. R. Tolkien: A Descriptive Bib-*

liography (1993). Other books he has edited include *The Dragon Path: Collected Tales of Kenneth Morris* (1995) and a reissue of E. A. Wyke-Smith's *The Marvellous Land of Snergs* (1996), a children's book originally published in 1927 that provided impetus for Tolkien's *The Hobbit*.

Nobody had ever won the Hugo and Nebula Awards for Best Novel two years in a row, until **Orson Scott Card** received them for *Ender's Game* and its sequel, *Speaker for the Dead*, in 1986 and 1987. *Xenocide* (1991) and *Children of the Mind* (1996) continued the series, and a new novel in the Ender's series, titled *Ender's Shadow,* was published in August 1999 (Tor Books). *Ender's Game* is currently in development as a film, with Card as screenwriter. Perhaps Card's most innovative work is his American fantasy series The Tales of Alvin Maker, whose first five volumes, *Seventh Son, Red Prophet, Prentice Alvin, Alvin Journeyman,* and *Heartfire,* are set in a magical version of the American frontier. Card has written two books on writing: *Character and Viewpoint* and *How to Write Science Fiction and Fantasy,* the latter of which won a Hugo Award in 1991, and has taught writing courses at several universities and workshops. He lives with his family in Greensboro, North Carolina.

Charles de Lint is a full-time writer and musician who presently makes his home in Ottawa, Canada, with his wife MaryAnn Harris, an artist and musician. His most recent books are the novel *Forests of the Heart* (Tor Books, 2000) and *Triskell Tales,* an illustrated collection of short stories (Subterranean Press, 2000). Other recent publications include a trade paperback reprint of his novel *Svaha* (Orb, 2000) as well as mass market editions of his novel *Someplace to Be Flying* (Tor Books, 1999) and *Moonlight and Vines,* a third collection of Newford stories which recently won the World Fantasy Award (Tor Books, 2000). For more information about his work, visit his website at www.charlesdelint.com.

Lisa Goldstein, Hugo, Nebula, and World Fantasy Award finalist, has published eight novels, the most recent being *Dark Cities Underground* from Tor. Her novel *The Red Magician* won the American Book Award for Best Paperback, and her short story collection, *Travellers in Magic* (Tor Books, 1994), was highly acclaimed. Her short fiction appears regularly in many publications, including *Asimov's*. She lives in Oakland, California, with her husband and their cute dog Spark.

Glenn Herdling discovered J. R. R. Tolkien in 1978, when he and two friends adapted *The Hobbit* into a comic book to help fund their eighth-grade trip to Washington D.C. As reference for the characters, he consulted the J. R. R. Tolkien calendars illustrated by the Brothers Hildebrandt. That experience led him on the path to fulfill two ambitions in life: to work in the comic book industry, and to meet and work alongside Greg and Tim Hildebrandt. While still attending Bucknell University in 1986, he began his comic book career at Marvel Comics as an editorial intern. In 1995, he left Marvel to take a job as Creative Director at the studio of the Hildebrandt brothers.

Tim and Greg Hildebrandt were virtually unknown as artists when they won the opportunity to illustrate the 1976 Ballantine calendar based on J. R. R. Tolkien's The Lord of the Rings. They went on to illustrate the Tolkien calendars for the next two years, with the 1978 calendar selling more than one million copies. They then illustrated the bestselling novel by Terry Brooks, *The Sword of Shanarra*. For the movies, they painted a poster for a 1979 re-release of *Barbarella*, the 1981 fantasy film *The Clash of the Titans,* and the world-famous poster for *Star Wars*. The Hildebrandts then went on to write (with Jerry Nichols) and illustrate their epic fantasy novel, *Urshurak*. Their most recent artbook, *Star Wars: The Art of Greg and Tim Hildebrandt,* was released in stores on November 17, 1997. The next one, *Greg and Tim Hildebrandt: The Tolkien Years,* will be published in 2001 by Watson-Guptill.

Terri Windling is a writer, editor, painter, and a six-time winner of the World Fantasy Award, as well as a passionate advocate of fantasy literature and mythic arts. As an author, she has published *The Wood Wife* (winner of the Mythopoeic Award), *A Midsummer Night's Faery Tale, The Winter Child, The Raven Queen,* and others, as well as a regular column on folklore and myth in *Realms of Fantasy* magazine. As an editor, she has created numerous anthologies, many of them in partnership with Ellen Datlow, including *the Snow White, Blood Red* adult fairy tales series, *The Year's Best Fantasy & Horror* annual volumes, *Sirens, The Armless Maiden,* the Borderland series (for teenagers) and *A Wolf at the Door* (for children). Previously the Fantasy Editor for Ace Books, she has been a Consulting Fantasy Editor for the Tor Books fantasy line since 1985.